## More Praise for *Stop Guessing*

"*Stop Guessing* presents a way of tackling hard problems. It is not a recipe book—rather, it identifies a set of behaviors that are essential to be successful at cracking those problems that do not readily submit to guessing as a viable solution. These behaviors are not difficult to learn but are essential when dealing with those frustrating challenges. No, you will not work miracles, but some might think that you do! This book is now on my reading list for all my students, as it will enable them to be more effective in their future careers."

—**Malcom McCulloch, Professor, Engineering Science, University of Oxford**

"I'd recommend this book to anyone involved in industrial problem solving. This approach should help readers get to the right answer quickly and with much less wasted effort."

—**Tim Ridgman, Course Director, Institute for Manufacturing, University of Cambridge**

"Having known Nat for fifteen years, I know he possesses a deep passion for solving problems, especially those more difficult and previously unsolved. In *Stop Guessing* he addresses the worthy cause and power of leveraging our human capital and capability to convert from firefighting to proactive and permanent solutions by leveraging people's potential as problem solvers. He effectively addresses the inhibitors to and realities of owning and embracing the solution. He embraces the art of the possible."

—**Greg Smith, Executive Vice President, Supply Chain, US, Wal-Mart Stores Inc.**

"I am so in awe of how Nat's mind works to create solutions to really challenging issues. I am so glad he took the time to share what he knows with us through *Stop Guessing*."

—**Diana Chapman, coauthor of *The 15 Commitments of Conscious Leadership* and cofounder of the Conscious Leadership Group**

"Vigorous, optimistic, and approachable. Nat shows us a robust approach that can empower people to take a confident, active role in solving problems. Readers who master this approach will save time and money and improve their self-esteem."

—**Dan Rosenthal, Radiologist, Massachusetts General Hospital**

# STOP
## GUESSING

# STOP
## GUESSING

### THE 9 BEHAVIORS OF GREAT
### PROBLEM SOLVERS

**Nat Greene**

Berrett–Koehler Publishers, Inc.
*a BK Business book*

**Berrett-Koehler Publishers, Inc.**
1333 Broadway, Suite 1000
Oakland, CA 94612-1921
Tel: (510) 817-2277    Fax: (510) 817-2278    www.bkconnection.com

**Ordering Information**

**Quantity sales.** Special discounts are available on quantity purchases by corporations, associations, and others. For details, contact the "Special Sales Department" at the Berrett-Koehler address above.

**Individual sales.** Berrett-Koehler publications are available through most bookstores. They can also be ordered directly from Berrett-Koehler: Tel: (800) 929-2929; Fax: (802) 864-7626; www.bkconnection.com

**Orders for college textbook/course adoption use.** Please contact Berrett-Koehler: Tel: (800) 929-2929; Fax: (802) 864-7626.

**Orders by U.S. trade bookstores and wholesalers.** Please contact Ingram Publisher Services, Tel: (800) 509-4887; Fax: (800) 838-1149; E-mail: customer. service@ingrampublisherservices.com; or visit www.ingrampublisherservices.com/ Ordering for details about electronic ordering.

Berrett-Koehler and the BK logo are registered trademarks of Berrett-Koehler Publishers, Inc.

Printed in Canada

Berrett-Koehler books are printed on long-lasting acid-free paper. When it is available, we choose paper that has been manufactured by environmentally responsible processes. These may include using trees grown in sustainable forests, incorporating recycled paper, minimizing chlorine in bleaching, or recycling the energy produced at the paper mill.

Library of Congress Cataloging-in-Publication Data
Greene, Nat, author.
Stop guessing : the 9 behaviors of great problem solvers / Nat Greene.
Description: First Edition. | Oakland : Berrett-Koehler Publishers, Inc., [2017]
LCCN 2016053592 | ISBN 9781626569867 (pbk.)
LCSH: Problem solving.
Classification: LCC BF449 .G74 2017 | DDC 153.4/3--dc23
LC record available at https://lccn.loc.gov/2016053592

First Edition
21  20  19  18  17    10  9  8  7  6  5  4  3  2  1

Cover: Wes Youssi, M.80 Design
Design and production: Seventeenth Street Studios
Icons: 9Pixel Designs
Copyeditor: Laurie Dunne
Index: Richard Evans
Author photo: Rick Ashley

*To dad, a great problem solving role model.*

# CONTENTS

# PREFACE

Have you ever encountered something in your life that wasn't working as well as you knew it could? Something costly, painful, or frustrating to your family or your business?

Perhaps your dishwasher doesn't dry your dishes well, and you're wasting your time hand drying them. Perhaps your business can't create enough of its product to meet customer demand. Perhaps your organizational processes are dysfunctional and unable to make good decisions. You may be trying to change bad habits in yourself or others, such as trying to eat better. Or maybe you are hoping to resolve a conflict with a colleague or loved one.

How many times have you or your organization tried to solve these hard problems and failed? How often do you build expensive workarounds, or just tolerate them as "part of life?" How many problems in your life have become so commonplace that you don't even notice them anymore?

Imagine a life in which you can see the problems around you and have confidence that you'll solve them. Imagine having great war stories of improving your life, your business, and your community by tackling the hardest problems that hold you back from your potential.

You can become an even better problem-solver. I want to help unleash your problem-solving potential and that of others so together we can form a powerful force for change.

## HOW THIS BOOK WILL HELP YOU

There are hundreds of books on problem-solving. Most of these focus on solving simple problems, or provide a step-by-step problem-solving method that the authors hope will help you progress on harder problems, like following a recipe.

When cooking an easy dish or solving an easy problem, a very specific step-by-step guide that you can robotically follow can lead you to victory, like with boiling an egg. But you'll notice that you can't take a totally untrained cook, hand them a recipe for a complicated gourmet dish, and expect it to come out very good. Great chefs demonstrate behaviors that set them apart from other cooks, allowing them to consistently create complex, novel dishes—even dishes others have never thought of before.

Great problem-solvers possess a specific set of behaviors that they apply to solve the hardest problems—the kinds others call "impossible" or have simply accepted as an unchangeable force of nature.

This book will help you understand the behaviors that great problem-solvers use to tackle the hardest problems with skill and panache, regardless of the industry or nature of the problem. These behaviors are universal and will help you to skillfully use whatever problem-solving methods you happen to know.

## WHAT PROBLEMS CAN YOU SOLVE WITH THE RIGHT BEHAVIORS?

Regardless of what you do in life and work, I bet you face problems that are important to you and that you fail to fully understand and resolve. You can change this if you recognize the strong problem-solving ability you already possess, enhance this ability, and then apply it to the tough problems around you. Here are some examples of problems you can work on by using the right behaviors:

- Technical problems at home, such as low water pressure or a door that won't close.

- Technical problems at work, such as critical assets breaking down or underperforming, faulty computer networks, or product quality problems.

- Organizational problems in your business, such as high employee turnover, low customer satisfaction, and logistics headaches.

- Personal health and behavioral problems, such as struggling to adopt new habits that will help you improve your health. Perhaps you want to lose weight or become more physically fit.

- Problems of personal conflict, in which two people that care about each other are upset and don't see eye-to-eye.

- Societal problems, such as global poverty or violence.

I believe the approaches I cover in this book are applicable to any hard problem, and I encourage you to think about hard problems in your life and draw parallels with the stories I share. I look forward to you adding to these stories with your own successes as you begin to solve hard problems.

This book is not a step-by-step guide. Instead, it will help you understand the behaviors you need to nurture if you want to be the greatest problem-solver you can be. Fulfilling your potential as a problem-solver requires practicing these behaviors, stretching yourself, and ideally, getting strong coaching. I have found no shortcuts or magical methods that can circumvent this. But with practice, you can fulfill that potential, and make both your life and community a better place.

# How to Be a Great Problem-Solver

Hard problems are everywhere around us. They lurk in all facets of our lives, unsolved. They make us suffer in ways that we recognize and ways that we have blocked out.

When we fail to solve these hard problems, we often learn to work around them, throw money and resources at them, or simply learn to live with them. These hard problems can persist so long that we or our organizations have long forgotten that they exist, even though they're costing us time and money. But while they are hard, they are not unconquerable. They can be solved.

This book will teach you about great problem-solving behaviors. These are the behaviors you need to solve practical problems—specifically, *hard* problems. If you are willing to apply and practice these behaviors as you approach hard problems, you will become a much better problem-solver, and the lives of everyone around you will flourish for it.

Take stock for a moment of some of the most frustrating situations in your life and work, and keep in mind the problems that you want to solve as you read. Perhaps at work you are having trouble gaining market share, or can't control costs in your department. Perhaps some process in the business or a critical asset is underperforming and you're getting endless phone calls about it. At home, you may be trying to get to the gym and can't do it consistently. Maybe you have conflict with a family member. Perhaps you simply have a dishwasher that's no longer really cleaning the dishes. Whatever problems you want to solve, think about how to apply each behavior to your efforts.

I'm incredibly passionate about helping to develop and nurture more great problem-solvers in the world. We certainly have no shortage of hard problems to solve in business, in our personal lives, and in society. It is frustrating to see deficient problem-solving all around. It's rampant. But you don't have to accept it.

I have often found it easier to illuminate what it takes to solve hard problems by looking at problems with physical systems that can be more easily understood and observed. This first story is one of my favorites.

## A WAR STORY: TOILET ROLLS AND SHRINK WRAP

Early in my career I worked as an industrial consultant and I found myself one morning standing in the middle of a large tissue paper mill. Behind me were several tissue machines: huge, noisy, hot things towering into the distance. They made giant rolls of tissue paper, taller than a person standing and much wider. In front of me were converting lines: They took these giant rolls and turned them into toilet rolls.

The converting process has been around for a long time, and consists of taking the giant rolls from the tissue machines and "rewinding" them onto a thin cardboard tube. These are then chopped up into individual toilet rolls by a large scary saw. If they're fancy rolls, they're individually wrapped in paper and sealed into a bag or case to be shipped out. If they are a low-cost product, many of them are put straight into a plastic bag as you might see in the grocery store. The whole process is fascinating, and it is well worth watching a video of it online.

In front of me that morning was a converting line that made high-end, branded toilet rolls in a nice fancy wrapper. They were being sold in plastic shrink-wrapped packaging for sale in bulk. I was looking at this line because there was a big problem with it: For some reason the plant could not make enough. You would think that toilet paper would be a fairly boring industry: steady demand, not much action. Well it turns out, as is often the case with these things, that when you look a little closer you'll find that a lot is going on.

The big drama was that marketing and sales had done a phenomenal job launching a new packaging format. Instead of selling toilet paper in packs of one, four, or 12, they had made a 20-pack. It was flying off the shelves and consumers loved the product. But the mill could not keep up with consumer demand. There were production problems that were spoiling the party, and the marketing dollars were already spent. That was why I was there. Business people hate missed sales.

The main problem on the line was the shrink-wrapper that took the stack of 20 rolls, put plastic around it, and then shrunk it all in a heat tunnel, creating a nice tight plastic wrap. If you wanted to make more you had to speed up the machine—that much was clear. But it was also clear to everyone that it simply wasn't possible to run this machine any faster. When you sped it up, anything you gained in speed was completely lost, because the machine kept malfunctioning. A pile of loose rolls would fly out of the machine with a bunch jumbled up in the shriveled plastic. Sometimes this would jam the line, and everything would need to be shut down as operators cleaned it up.

This was a well-known problem to the plant and everyone had worked on it. The shrink-wrapper supplier reps had come and gone, leaving a proposal for buying a new, improved machine. The maintenance guys had tried a number of things. The plant engineers had all tried to fix it, as well as the production team. The prevailing theory was that a mechanical arm that drew the plastic film over the stacked toilet rolls could not move faster. There was a strong consensus that nothing could be done and they would just have to continue to work hard through the weekends until demand dropped off, supplying as many 20-packs as possible.

The option to buy and install a new shrink-wrapping machine was seriously considered as a medium-term solution, but that would take a while to plan and then would involve moving a lot of equipment to get it in. The shrink-wrapper was, after all, trapped in the middle of all these converting lines with conveyors all over the place rushing toilet rolls here and there. No one wanted to lose a couple of weeks' production trying to get that to work. People were out of other useful ideas, and pretty demoralized. This is the sad state that most hard problems end up when people have gone through their list of guesses and failed to solve them.

People are conditioned to guess, and it takes training and skill that comes through guided practice to go beyond guessing. Above all, it requires a certain behavioral attitude that you will learn in this book. People are often reluctant to bring in outsiders, but they also hate weekly conference calls where they are asked why performance is not good enough. So I had an opportunity to take a shot at the problem.

The smart, knowledgeable people who had worked on the issue so far had been trained in a number of problem-solving approaches that relied on experience or guesswork, or sometimes both together. I had been trained not to guess, and when one stops guessing, real problem-solving begins.

I had listened to everyone's theories and guesses as to what was happening, pushed them out of my mind, and set to work studying the problem. On first pass the solution was not obvious. It was clearly a harder problem. I went into more depth, studied the failures in detail, observed how the process worked, engaged the local team to help me understand key technical points, and wrote out a variable tree (which I'll cover later) for what must be happening. I spent all morning and most of the afternoon working on the problem, and it felt like the solution was just out of reach, but close.

I methodically eliminated every critical variable except one. Understanding a consistent pattern of tearing, along with Newtonian physics, told me there *must* be an unintended force acting on the plastic, caused by something snagging the plastic film before it was correctly "shrunk" in the heater section. However, when we cleared out the machine there was nothing that could be in the way and nothing visible when watching the machine run from the side (you could not easily and safely see down the length of the line or from above or below). It was a real head-scratcher.

When I left for the night I reviewed the situation with the night-shift mechanic and asked for his help in figuring out the final part. I had eliminated everything except for this one mysterious force, and we knew that something during wrapping must be catching the plastic in a very specific area of the machine. But I wasn't yet sure how to observe this mysterious force in action.

I went back to my hotel and pondered the problem at dinner, in bed, at breakfast, and while driving back and towards the facility. When I got in early to catch the night-shift mechanic he came bouncing up to me and handed me a bolt. The problem was solved! We stepped over to a quiet part of the factory floor and he told me the story.

He had been working near the machine the night before when a problem had cropped up. Some errant toilet rolls had jammed part of the machine, so he had fixed it and gotten things running again. He then decided to dry cycle the machine to ensure everything was in alignment before starting production. This involved removing the plastic wrap and stopping the in-feed of toilet rolls.

Then he had a great idea: He decided that this was a good time to "smell the problem." Previously, we had observed the empty machine while it was off, and we had observed it running, but while it was full of plastic and toilet rolls. He decided to safely, but closely, observe the machine while it was dry cycling, paying close attention to the very specific area we had determined must be the source of the mystery force.

He increased the machine's speed, above the "DO NOT RUN FASTER THAN" level that every operator had come to accept. Now that he was running the machine empty, he had a clear view of that section, so he shone a flashlight into the machine as he watched.

These machines are pretty noisy and they vibrate a lot, as they have many big moving parts. And as the vibrating got a little more intense with higher speed, he saw *something* wiggle its way into the chute. Something small, but *definitely there.* He knelt, bewildered, with this trickle of adrenaline starting to course through him—maybe this was it! It was definitely in the right area, and definitely looked like it could snag the plastic film. But what was it?

He decided to speed up the machine even more and look again: There it was, protruding even further. It was shaking, too. As one more experiment, he gradually slowed the machine down and the thing actually receded its way back into the hole. It became clear that the vibrations of the machine at higher speeds were causing the mystery object to vibrate its way through the hole and poke out into the chute and tear the shrink-wrap.

Resisting the urge to run, he shut down the machine, locked it out, opened up the panel in the general area of the mystery object, and peered inside with the flashlight. And there, sitting in a horizontal hole, was a loose bolt, perhaps mistakenly dropped in by routine maintenance years ago. He almost couldn't believe it was so simple.

He took the bolt out, closed the machine up, dry-cycled it again to check, and saw this time that no mystery object poked out into the chute. They were ready to rock. He brought the production supervisor over and together they tested out running the machine—with product this time—at full speed, and had hours of great production.

In the following months, their output was up over 25% and they were able to meet customer demand. Weekly production phone calls substituted groaning with high-fives. The success was so invigorating for everyone that the bolt became a symbol of powerful problem-solving.

This was a hard problem because it had resisted many attempts to solve it and been declared unsolvable. It also had a complex pattern of failure for such a seemingly simple issue: The plastic film was not in exactly the same place every time, the bolt did not vibrate and move in the same way every time, and these factors changed with the machine's speed. Finally, safely observing this was hard and "general observation" would not get you there. I know as I spent time looking at it myself while working out the critical issue, and others had probably spent dozens of hours doing the same.

Solving this problem required core problem-solving behaviors that I had learned, as well as help from the team. To successfully find the bolt, we had to know exactly what we were looking for. I cannot imagine anyone guessing that there might just be a loose bolt vibrating into the way at certain speeds.

What made the difference here? Instead of guessing, we rigorously measured the problem by employing the right problem-solving behaviors. We spent more time "smelling the problem"—understanding the symptoms of the problem itself and rigorously defining it—rather than thinking of causes or solutions. Instead of asking for more ideas or guesses from experts, we dug into the fundamental science behind the problem by exploring the mechanical forces that moved—or tore—the shrink-wrap. We kept our focus by relying only on facts to guide our decisions, and by investigating only the parts of the process that were directly relevant to our problem.

In this book you will learn the behaviors that have solved hard problems like this one. Hundreds and thousands of these problems exist in every business, in society, and in your personal life as well, and they destroy value and progress. They are frustrating and demoralizing. Most of them remain unseen or are hidden as a natural defense mechanism.

## LET'S SOLVE SOME HARD PROBLEMS

First, let me clarify what kinds of problems you're going to be solving. When I say "practical problems" I mean problems in systems or processes, man-made or natural. I don't mean problems of philosophy, such as "what is love?" I don't simply mean complex decisions, and I don't mean problems of innovation or strategy. I'm referring to problems in which a system or process is operating in a way that we don't want it to, and our lives will be better if the problematic behavior is solved. These problems might include a stubborn waistline, a computer that shuts down intermittently, a public policy that is not achieving its intended goal, or a troublesome relationship.

An easy problem might be one where your car suddenly starts coasting to a stop, and you hear the engine sputtering. Turns out you were too wrapped up in the latest podcast to notice that your fuel gauge was empty, so you need to get fuel for the car. The vast majority of problems are like this. You use methods you're used to: You use your experience and intuition, and you guess. Because most problems are easy, one of your guesses is often right, and so this approach is practical and efficient. But what happens when you've tried the quick, obvious things that come to mind, and you still haven't solved the problem?

A *hard* problem is one where the solution is deeply hidden or obscure. These problems tend to exist in more complex systems or processes, and have often stubbornly resisted previous attempts to solve them. Our conventional approaches to solving easy problems do not work for solving hard ones.

Some examples of hard problems that I'll discuss in this book include a failing chemical processor that cost hundreds of millions of dollars, a losing baseball team without the budget for star players, and the scourge of poverty in sub-Saharan Africa. These hard problems can be tedious to illustrate in fine detail, so I'll cover them briefly in the book. (For those interested, you can view more detailed case studies of these problems at www.stopguessingbook.com.)

The examples are mostly from my personal experience, along with a few that I have read about, so they'll be weighted heavily to problems I encounter as a consultant in industry, the problems I have run into around my house, and those I deal with as a friend, a husband, and as a father. I believe strongly that these same behaviors can be applied to problems of almost any kind, and I have seen evidence of the behaviors working well in other hard problems that people have solved around the world. But in order to be accurate and clear, I will stick primarily to the examples I know best.

## HOW BECOMING A GREAT
## PROBLEM-SOLVER CAN CHANGE YOUR LIFE

Many people accept the world the way it is, and don't see the incredible potential that is locked behind hard problems. But throughout history, solving the hardest problems facing humanity has been at the root of much of our economic, medical, and social progress. Imagine for a moment a world in which a few million great problem-solvers are on hand to deploy to these problems. A world of great problem-solving will yield incredible economic and social impact for each of us.

You may be able to imagine how solving problems in your operations, human resources department, sales and marketing, and research and development can help your business's bottom line. But when businesses solve hard problems that are holding them back, they often become far more resource efficient: They are able to waste less materials and energy, fuel, and carbon, and that helps everyone. A colleague of mine helped a large industrial plant save millions of dollars in energy costs by helping them convert from burning natural gas to using bark from the trees—in a few weeks and without added capital cost. In the same stroke, she eliminated so much fossil-fuel burning that it offset the lifetime carbon output of my entire team and all their families.

Imagine being able to thoroughly understand and change undesirable behaviors in your life or those of your friends coming to you for help. If you're able to understand what drives your overeating, procrastination, or anger, you can alter key levers in your thinking and environment to achieve victory. Without this understanding, you're depending on hope—and hope is not a strategy.

Developing your problem-solving skills can also lead to tremendous improvements in your relationships. I'm at the age now where some of my friends are having serious marital problems, or even getting divorced. Some will discuss this with me, and what I consistently learn is that their marriages are falling apart because of problems that cropped up 10 years earlier, and simply weren't confronted. Instead, they festered and built resentment, and by the time the couples started really talking, they had drifted apart. They didn't have the skills to solve these problems before they became too big, so the couples had often lost the will to tackle them and they seemed impossibly difficult. Some people are just not meant to be together and other change over time, but the application of great problem-solving behaviors would certainly help, whatever they decide for their futures.

When you're a great problem-solver, you can help your organization or family make better decisions and reduce conflict. Many heated disagreements seem to stem from people having different opinions over the best course of action, and trying to use social capital to compel others to trust them over someone else. Instead, imagine if you understood completely how each decision would affect the bottom line you all want, and were able to tell the story clearly and decisively. I've found that great problem-solving makes developing alignment as easy as it can be.

These skills can even help you overcome bias in others. The main bias I suffered from in my early twenties was that I was seen as being too young to help a business. People believed I lacked the maturity and experience to add value. Because I had developed great problem-solving skills, I was able to help business leaders clearly see the reasoning behind a great decision, instead of rely on the "authority" of experience that I did not have. Instead of being seen as an immature young person, I was seen as a helpful problem-solver, and respected for it.

## WHY PEOPLE CAN'T SOLVE HARD PROBLEMS

Most people guess when they try to solve problems. You may not believe that you do, but any time you come up with a list of possible root causes, or a "hypothesis," or anything that you need to test before you are certain it's the root cause, you are guessing. The good news is that most problems are pretty easy: We solve them all the time, and we may not even be aware that we're solving problems. Humanity got to 7 billion people by solving most of the problems it ran into—some of them hard, many of them easy. Conventional, guess-based approaches will work fine for these easy problems, but they'll run into trouble with hard ones.

Here's where most folks go wrong: Often, people use the same guessing methods they apply to easy problems to try to tackle hard ones, and they get steamrolled. It's like sending your high school basketball team up against the Michael Jordan-era Chicago Bulls—it's just not going to work, and you're going to have to take your game to the next level if you want to solve them. I want to help you understand the behaviors you need to play like an all-star problem-solver.

There are some very simple problem-solving methods, such as Five Whys, that will help you to guess with greater focus.[1] There are also some others that have pages upon pages of steps to follow, and there are many books peddling many of these methods. But solving hard problems is about far more than having a good problem-solving method. Imagine trying to walk into surgery armed only with a handbook, one that is designed to guide you through any kind of surgery with a single step-by-step approach. It's obvious in any other context: You need to know how to use your brain and make decisions in the field in order to be successful at surgery.

Likewise, when solving hard problems you need to learn how to draw on the right behaviors in the right circumstances, and I have found that most people are never taught about great problem-solving behaviors before they're expected to solve hard problems. It's really no mystery why people struggle so much with it.

With the right skills and behaviors, we can solve hard personal problems such as chronic illnesses, bad habits, and stubborn extra weight. We can solve technical problems at home and at work, from glitches in your car to outages at massive refineries. As a society, we can solve global systemic problems, such as many diseases, economic risks, violence, and environmental contamination. Our lives and the world can become a much better place.

Without a doubt, many of the hardest problems facing the world require more than just a few smart folks to understand the root cause behind what's solving them. Some will require great scientific innovations or discoveries; some will require the mustering of significant resources. I have been solving hard problems for a long time and still shrug my shoulders whenever somebody asks me how to create peace in the Middle East. But every unsolved problem *is* bottlenecked by not understanding the root cause at a fundamental level, and every single one needs some great problem-solvers to crack it.

To become a great problem-solver, you'll need to practice these behaviors on easier problems, using a structured method to guide you and, ideally, a coach to provide feedback and a sounding board. But the most important step to take is to get out there and start solving problems.

What hard problems are you living with? Which ones have you tried and failed to solve? Where have you given up or worked around a problem at great expense? Now is the time to do something about that: We're going to go solve some hard problems.

## WHAT TO EXPECT

This book will help you understand the behaviors that great problem-solvers use to solve hard problems with skill and panache, and what holds us back from applying them. In the first nine chapters, we'll discuss each of these behaviors, along with illustrative stories and practical guidance.

**Stop guessing.** This means stop brainstorming and stop just trying things out. After a few benign guesses at a hard problem, you'll realize it's hard and it's time to try something new. But nature abhors a vacuum, so if you don't have other behaviors at hand, you'll revert to your old ones. That's where the other eight behaviors come in: They will help you to stop guessing at solutions and instead measure the problem.

**Smell the problem.** Get out from the chair and get in the field, using your natural senses and tools available to you to develop a strong pattern of failure. This doesn't mean burying yourself in streams of data: It means asking relevant questions about the specific problem. This behavior can solve some moderately difficult problems right away, and will be critical to solving hard ones.

**Embrace your ignorance.** Most people try to solve problems using the knowledge they already have about a process, but it's what you don't know that lies between you and the solution. Often we are afraid to admit our ignorance in front of others in order to preserve our reputation. Great problem-solvers not only admit their ignorance but also embrace it and ask questions others might find "stupid," to shatter old assumptions about the problem.

**Know what problem you're solving.** Often, people work on the wrong problem entirely by making some implicit assumption about what's causing it. Great problem-solvers invest time upfront to make sure the problem they're working on is well defined, measurable as a variable, and represents precisely what is wrong with the system or process.

**Dig into the fundamentals.** This means learning how the process works, both by understanding the process itself and by understanding some of the fundamental science behind it. By focusing on what controls your problem, you'll be able to limit your digging to the parts of the process and the science that are relevant, rather than trying to wrap your arms around the entire thing at once.

**Don't rely on experts.** Utilizing subject-matter experts is critical to understanding a complex system and its underlying functionality and science. Unfortunately, most people delegate responsibility for solving the problem to these subject-matter experts, rather than driving the problem-solving process themselves. Sometimes internal and external experts aren't well positioned to solve the problem for you, and great problem-solvers always view experts as collaborators rather than saviors.

**Believe in a simple solution.** When confronting complex problems, it can be comforting to believe that the solution will be complex as well. But by not believing in a simple solution, people often give up long before they've gone through the rigor required to find the simple solution that lies at the root cause, to great cost and detriment. Great problem-solvers will have the belief and tenacity to keep solving until they've found the true root cause, and will be able to most easily and economically implement the simple solution that emerges.

**Make fact-based decisions.** Avoid making opinion-based decisions: Anything that relies on a vote, on authority, or on some subjective ranking system of what decision to make is one of these opinion-based decisions, and it leads problem-solvers astray. Great problem-solvers insist on using only facts to make decisions in problem-solving, and relentlessly verify what they are told. They check data streams to ensure that what they're observing represents reality.

**Stay on target.** When problem-solvers dive deep into a problem, they too frequently seek to expand the number of possible root causes, so they can test them. They attempt to wrap their arms around the entire process and everything that could be causing it. This wastes time and resources, and is unlikely to find the true root cause among hundreds or thousands of potential causes. Great problem-solvers measure the drivers that most immediately control the problem in order to determine whether those subvariables are in control, and in doing so are able to quickly eliminate most possible root causes and avenues of inquiry without having to dive deeper into them. This keeps them efficiently on-track, enabling them to find the root cause.

**Choose your method.** Great problem-solvers often use structure in order to stay on track and consistently apply these behaviors. In Chapter 10, "Choose Your Method," you will learn how to assess different problem-solving methods by understanding their underlying elements. Strong problem-solving methods will discourage guessing, provide lots of structure to develop a pattern of failure, and guide you to understand how the process works.

**CHAPTER 1**

# Stop Guessing

*I never guess. It is a shocking habit—destructive to the
logical faculty.*[1]

—SHERLOCK HOLMES, IN *SIGN OF THE FOUR*

Unlike Mr. Holmes, the rest of us guess sometimes. When we face
something that's broken or any problem in our lives, our frontal
cortex lights up with one or dozens of ideas of what might be
wrong and how to fix it. We might jot these down and quickly
get to work.

Guessing is a natural brain function. In our evolutionary history, humans had to quickly make decisions with very limited
information. We had problems such as "What tool should I use to
deal with this saber-toothed tiger trying to separate me from my
larynx?" Spending time studying your problem and finding the
root cause behind your unfortunate conundrum was a behavior
that natural selection quickly pruned from our family trees thousands of years ago.

And that natural tendency to guess is reinforced throughout
our lives. In school, we are rewarded by teachers for being the
first to raise our hands with a guess to the answer of a question. In order to promote self-esteem, teachers reward wrong
answers, too: "good guess!" We're discouraged from simply saying, "I don't know."

In business we also naturally default to guessing. We're encouraged by others who crave quick action when problems arise—regardless of the quality. Spending hours staring at data or a broken machine can be seen as slow or lazy, whereas the employee that "rolls up their sleeves" and immediately tries something is seen as heroic.

I don't know when I first came across this issue, but the first example I can recall was while I was in a factory in Georgia. A piece of equipment had broken down, stopping the production line. A mechanic spent 8 hours changing a half-dozen parts until he got it back up and running. After production was back online, he told a story that has become very familiar to me: "I ripped it open and changed out this part, but that didn't fix it. And I also had to change this *other* part, and *then...* " He was celebrated by the leadership team for his tenacity and effort, but nobody asked whether he could have brought the plant online much faster by actually investigating what the root cause was. And it seems highly unlikely that four or five parts all failed at once.

This isn't problem-solving. It's solution-guessing. Truly solving the problem involves understanding what's wrong and why it happened, through investigation and understanding—not by spending days or weeks testing different guesses until, hopefully, one works.

## WHY GUESSING FAILS

Through both nature and nurture, guessing has become a foundation of our problem-solving skill set. And guessing helps us resolve many of our problems, but only the easy ones. When a light bulb is off, we guess that flipping the switch will turn it on. If that doesn't work, we guess that changing the bulb will get the job done. If *that* doesn't work, we typically scowl at the light as we flip the switch a few more times, and then go check the breaker-box: Aha! We flip the breaker, check the light, and bask in its glow.

What does the IT engineer at your company say when someone calls them to tell them their computer isn't working? "Is it plugged in?" Often asking three or four such questions solves the problem. If you suddenly start vomiting, you might guess that it has something to do with what you ate last night—and you might be right. But you might not.

Solution-guessing is a hit-or-miss technique. When a problem has two or three potential root causes, and when testing them is cheap and quick, it's entirely appropriate. But these are easy problems. Most persistent problems in our lives aren't easy by definition: They would not persist if they were easy to fix.

What would we do if the breaker wasn't flipped? Or if it flipped again after a few minutes, plunging us once more into darkness? Or if our light bulb blows out repeatedly? At this point, it's time to realize we don't have an easy problem on our hands, and guessing won't solve it. If you don't have a strong problem-solving skill set, you have three options: You might keep guessing, hoping you might resolve it. You might call in an expert—in this case an electrician—and they'll be able to use their experience to make an "educated guess," which can move easy problems along. But when that fails, you'll probably just cough up the money to replace whatever appears to not be working, or just live with it.

When you're facing a problem of moderate difficulty, there may be something like 50 potential root causes. Perhaps you've developed intermittent sneezing fits, or your motorcycle engine occasionally stalls out in the middle of the highway, or you're not making any progress on your diet. At work, perhaps your emissions are too close to the regulatory limit for comfort, or you suspect your sales force is not selling as hard as they can because they believe the supply chain won't be able to meet their commitments to the customer. If you are really good at guessing—perhaps with the help of some colleagues—you might come up with 30 potential causes.

It takes time and resources to test every guess. With a long list, it's likely you'll waste lots of both. Worse, there's a good chance that the root cause isn't on your list, and you have no way of knowing until you've completed testing the entire thing, which might take months. What will you do next? Perhaps get a bigger group together to create a longer list of guesses?

Then you've got hard problems. These are the kinds of problems that might have hundreds or *thousands* of potential causes. The actual root cause is obscure or hidden. Shearing pipes in your water pipes might be due to invasive corrosive bacteria introduced at the local river. Your trouble sleeping might be caused by an allergy to yellow-6 dye in your macaroni. You are unlikely to be able to guess the causes to these, and *trying to guess wastes a lot of time.* Trying to implement some of these guesses is a shot in the dark and quickly uses up huge amounts of resources. Your brainstorming efforts will generate a list of some dozens of "possible root causes." You'll tirelessly grind through them and, months later, have nothing to show for it. Worse yet, with all of the random changes you have made, you've probably created new problems.

Brainstorming might be useful in situations where creativity is required. However, solving hard problems is not one of these. Rather than having one person guess at something, brainstorming is gathering a lot of people together to group-guess, which adds the further complication of groupthink and politics. Often this guessing is covered up with an elaborate "process" for prioritizing the guesses. You can do better than this.

At one food processing plant, they were making a product in a plastic cup with a seal on top—the sort you tear off in order to eat. Customers were getting moldy food because the seals weren't working properly. You can imagine this was a fairly important problem for brand and food safety reasons. This corporation had invested heavily in Lean and Six Sigma techniques and had a sizeable organization dedicated to solving this problem. When we arrived, they had used a Fishbone-Diagram approach to identify over 200 potential causes and ideas to fix them (this was clearly a pretty hard problem).[2] On the surface, they had taken a very structured approach, but in reality, it's what I call "structured guessing." Any time you "come up with" many things to check that could be the cause, **you are guessing** (see Table 1.1).

If you get from someone a list of 10 "potential" root causes, they *don't know what's happening.* If you've come up with 200, you have no idea at all what's happening. This number of ideas is far too many to search through with any reasonable effort: An individual or team is going to run out of time, resources, and energy long before they get through the list. And worse, when a team doesn't understand a problem or the system behind it, odds are good that the true root cause isn't even on the list. This is why guessing won't solve these problems.

| Table 1.1: What people say to cover up guessing. |
| --- |
| I have a hypothesis! |
| I have a theory! |
| I'm pretty sure X is true. |
| We listed the most likely options. |
| The group voted on this one. |
| I'm not guessing, I'm taking action. |
| I was right, so it couldn't have been a guess. |
| Our experience suggests… |

Over a period of 4 months the food processing plant had invested one year of work and $200K trying out about one-third of these ideas, and they'd not gotten close to solving the problem. They had actually created new problems for their production line as they installed new drive-chains for the sealing equipment and made many other changes. When you make 50 changes to a production line, and only one in 10 causes a new problem, you've still created five new problems.

Taking an approach designed to solve hard problems took care of this issue in a few weeks, and demonstrated that the root cause wasn't on the original list. Not a single guess was made in that entire effort. But "structured guessing" had cost the business a lot, including time and money. We'll have a closer look at this example in Chapter 8, "Make Fact-Based Decisions," and Chapter 9, "Stay on Target."

## THE CURSE OF LUCK

Imagine Sherlock Holmes trying to catch a serial killer with guessing. "Maybe it was the butler!" So we throw the butler in jail, but the serial killer strikes again! "Perhaps it was that shady fellow!" Six murders later we have seven more people behind bars waiting for the circus to end, but Sherlock has another hunch. "Maybe it was the chief of police!" At that point everyone rolls their eyes and tells Sherlock that he'd better not quit his day job. The practice of guessing so obviously fails in detective work that it's almost shocking that we guess when we have important problems to solve.

But let's say you guess, and you get lucky: You found a solution and implemented it effectively. You may or may not have spent a lot of time and resources on it. Unfortunately, some bad side effects come with this rare victory.

First, you've reinforced the habit of guessing in your mind or in your organization, fooled yourself into thinking it's a good strategy and is going to work again, and made the habit harder to break in the future. Whether or not it works, it's easy, and we find comfort in that.

Second, you haven't developed a deeper understanding of whatever you're trying to fix, whether it's yourself, a process, or a machine. Instead of spending time building some knowledge of the fundamentals that you can use in the future—new problems are popping up all the time—you've spent your time guessing and checking. So next time there's a problem, you're back to square one.

Third, and perhaps most importantly, you're not becoming a better problem-solver. While guessing might eventually get the job done for problems of moderate difficulty (although at great cost), you rob yourself or your team of critical skills development. When you get to truly hard problems, you're going to need all of the skill you can get: If you don't practice using the right behaviors and method to solve moderate problems then you will never master them, and you're going to get shellacked when you try to tackle the hard ones.

## GUESSING IN POPULAR PROBLEM-SOLVING METHODS

Many businesses teach their people structured methods to help them solve problems. Structure can be very helpful in certain stages of the problem-solving method, adding rigor to defining the problem and finding a pattern of failure. These are important steps beyond simple guessing or brainstorming, and they are critical to quickly solving problems of fairly easy or moderate difficulty. Many direct the problem-solver to spend significant effort studying the problem *in situ,* which is a significant step in the right direction away from solution-guessing at a table, in a conference room, or behind a computer. Understanding the pattern of failure allows a problem-solver to quickly eliminate some of the root causes by testing them against the pattern of failure. This can shorten the list of guesses and accelerate progress on some moderately difficult problems.

Where most of these structured methods break down is that they ultimately resort to guessing to determine what root causes may be. While they can help you solve some moderate problems, you still depend on the hope that your guessed cause is on the list you developed. Hard problems are immune to them.

For example, consider a classic problem-solving methodology such as the PackCorp Scientific Approach, which was popular in the 1960s and was one of the first to introduce rigorous problem definitions.[3] Its method has the following nine steps:

1. Pick a problem

2. Get knowledge

3. Organize knowledge

4. Refine knowledge

5. Digest

6. **Produce ideas**

7. Rework ideas

8. Put ideas to work

9. Repeat the process

Steps 2 through 5 are dedicated to studying a pattern of failure, which was a breakthrough in problem-solving. But step 6, "produce ideas," depends on insight, inspiration, and brainstorming to determine potential root causes.

When you look at most popular problem-solving approaches, you'll find that they devolve into structured-guessing at some point. Many have steps such as, "develop possible root causes" or "deduce probable causes." Whenever we develop some list of possible root causes, we're guessing, even if it's structured guessing. Some of these guessing steps are disguised as "forming hypotheses" or other seemingly scientific approaches. Many of these methods are designed to focus on simple problems quickly, where one needs to just organize guesses—Five Whys is great for this. For hard problems, though, the likelihood that you'll include the true root cause in the list of "possible root causes" that you guess is tiny.

For sufficiently complex systems, it's inconceivable that one or a group of human minds could comprehend it in order to effectively guess the right root cause. The Fault Tree Analysis for Boeing's 747, which lists known potential causes of catastrophic in-flight failure, has *thousands* of elements.[4] In some in-flight failures, like TWA Flight 800, the root cause is not on the prebuilt FTA—there are just too many possibilities.

The structure that comes with some of these methods can accelerate problem-solving for easy and moderate problems by pointing them in the right direction. To solve truly hard problems, you'll need to use a method that doesn't involve guessing in any step. There are methods that avoid guessing, but they are rare. You should find one you like. The one I'm most familiar with can be found in Chapter 10, "How to Choose Your Method," along with some guidance on how to pick the method that's right for you.

## DEALING WITH GUESSING

Let's be honest: You're going to have guesses. If you're working with a team, *they're* going to have guesses. That's fine, it's natural. These guesses are going to bounce around and might distract you if you're not experienced at solving hard problems.

If you or your team seem are distracted by guessing, I've found it useful not to suppress it but to write it down and get it out of your system. Put it in an envelope and *ignore it.* If in the end, you were right, pat yourself on the back.

This is actually a great exercise with a team: Get everyone to write down what they think the root cause to your tough problem is, and put them all in a box that you lock tight. Better yet, get them to write down what they think the root cause is, why, and what data they'd use to convince everyone else.

After the problem is solved, if your guess ended up being right, ask yourself if you had the data on hand to be able to decisively convince others to prioritize your guess over theirs. Until we actually *know* the root cause, there's no effective way to prioritize different guesses, and the best guess is likely to be lost.

## IT'S NATURAL TO GUESS, AND YOU CAN STOP

I've been fortunate to work with some of the brightest talent in the world fresh out of universities such as MIT, Cornell, Queens, Oxford, and Cambridge. These graduates are brilliant young people and most have technical degrees of some sort that make them very familiar with solving problems. They have a deep scientific foundation. They've synthesized complex chemicals and built robots. But when they're faced with their first hard practical problem, I've found that they all guess and flail. But once they recognize how the compulsion to guess inhibits progress, they can handle hard problems with panache.

Great problem-solvers resist the temptation to guess at every stage of the process. Guessing is a tough habit to break, so get started!

## NOW: STOP GUESSING

Remember, your brain is going to guess. When these guesses happen, recognize them for what they are and then let them roll off you like rain. If you're really struggling to let them go, write them down on a piece of paper and stick it in an envelope or a box. You can look at it later to see how close you got.

CHAPTER 2

# Smell the Problem

*An essential part of seeing clearly is finding the willing-
ness to look closely and go beyond our own ideas.*[1]
—CHERI HUBER, *THERE IS NOTHING WRONG WITH YOU*

All too often, attempting to solve hard problems is done almost
exclusively at a desk, in a conference room, or behind a computer. Or, if you're in the field, you're just taking action, trying
out different solutions. For problems of any significant difficulty,
you need to start with your hands in your pockets, and your
senses open. **You need to get out there and study the problem in detail.**

As a problem-solver of any system—be it a machine, a circuit,
a code base, your body, or your habits—your mission is to smell
the problem. Get out there and thoroughly describe the problem
in detail with all of your senses: Record your observations of
when and where the problem is occurring. Get the information
you need to understand the problem, but don't just get reams of
data that you're hoping will help you guess the solution—getting to the root cause of the problem comes later. Go back to
smelling the problem more as you need to.

## GOOD PROBLEM-SOLVERS ARE PROBLEM-SMELLERS

People have been solving problems since the early days of human
civilization. Let's use an example everyone is familiar with: going
to the doctor. In the days of Hippocrates in ancient Greece,

doctors had little technology at hand to diagnose illnesses. Back then before lab testing, doctors would poke and prod, bend an arm, listen to your stomach or chest. They'd even smell wounds for gangrene and infection, smell your breath or your stool to learn more about gastrointestinal problems. They were very rigorously studying the problem and the patterns of failure.

In modern times, good doctors study the problem before coming up with potential diagnoses or even running more complex or expensive tests. They'll also poke and prod you. They ask you to move, bend, twist, cough, and report how you feel. They listen with a stethoscope, and take your temperature, blood pressure, and pulse. They want to know what you ate or what your physical activity has been. If the stakes are high or the cause is hard to pin down, they will schedule an X-ray, lab work, or an MRI, but only after first using simpler methods.

Doctors will also ask you to keep a log of what you eat or your physical activity if you have a chronic or recurring problem that they can't diagnose by looking at your body. You'll write what you ate, what you did, and how you felt, with an eye to the specific problem. Great problem-solvers will make sure their data, too, is robust and problem-specific.

Psychologists and therapists do the same thing. They have a battery of questions. They dig into your past. Good ones may spend hours dissecting your mind before attempting to diagnose. It's a long way from your friend telling you that you need a better attitude, after listening to you for a few minutes and jumping to a solution.

You can do this, too. A friend of mine has asked me whether he was drinking too much and if he has a problem with alcohol. Now I don't think I am particularly qualified to make this judgment, but I can help him look at what is actually going on. Most people have simply told him either, "don't worry about it," or "yes, you should drink less." How they have the information to draw that conclusion beats me. I have had him smell the problem by keeping a diary of how much he drinks and when, as well as noting his emotional state when doing so. Where it will lead I am not sure, but getting actual data will allow for progress on what could be a hard problem with serious consequences.

This approach, smelling the problem, can give you lots of insight about the nature of the problem you are experiencing. With simpler problems, establishing a strong pattern of failure can give you the solution on its own.

## HOW TO SMELL WELL

**Early on you'll want to smell the problem to develop a pattern of failure.** Where possible, understanding where the problem does and doesn't happen, when the problem started, and how often the problem occurs will generate critical insights for the problem-solving effort. For easy or fairly moderate problems, this pattern of failure can lead to the key insight that solves the problem or puts you just one step away.

A friend of mine was helping his mother understand why her car's push-to-talk (PTT) feature was malfunctioning. When she pushed the button and asked it to play Lady Gaga, it would some-times work great, and she could rock out. But intermittently, it would bring up the car's navigation feature. It was driving her up the wall (blessedly, only figuratively so). The car dealer and its shop couldn't figure it out, and had actually written it off as a software bug, a short circuit, or entirely nonexistent and all in mom's head. They wasted lots of time, nearly lost a customer, and even offered to replace the car, because they didn't smell the problem.

My friend, while visiting his mother one weekend, smelled the problem by repeatedly mashing the button and using all of his senses. A subtle pattern emerged: there were different numbers and tones of beeps just before navigation and just before music. He noted this, read the owner's manual with this knowledge, and learned that you needed to hold the PTT button for more than two seconds to access music. He instructed his mom and solved the problem permanently. Now of course others had read the manual before him, but just the section on the onboard computer was dozens of pages, and they didn't know what they were looking for.

There are literally dozens of problems like this that we encounter every year that waste our money, try our patience, and consume our time. Simply smelling the problem well can help you resolve them and lead a better life.

## DEVELOPING A PATTERN OF FAILURE

There are problem-solving methods that can help us add rigor and practice. They ask thought-provoking questions that guide you to collect information and look for very specific patterns, rather than shotgunning and looking at everything in the system. These vary in their level of rigor, detail, and prescription. In Chapter 10, "How to Choose Your Method," we'll discuss how to select some of these methods over others. For now, know that when you're dealing with hard problems, having guidance is extremely helpful, but not exhaustive. Hard problems tend to be unique, so use these as a guide rather than a recipe. As you develop insight, you'll come up with your own questions to ask.

I can provide some basic guidance on where to get started in developing a strong pattern of failure (see Table 2.1). Most generally, describe in detail the conditions in which a problem does and does not occur.

| Table 2.1: Questions to ask when smelling the problem. |
|---|
| What does the problem look like? |
| If you look closely, is it always the same every time? |
| When did you first see the problem? |
| What pattern do you notice if you look at the problem over time? |
| Where might you expect to see the same problem but don't? |

All of the questions in Table 2.1 are guides, not directions. Look at one occurrence and many together, when possible, and see what you discover. Again, you are not trying to guess the solution. You are simply trying to understand the facts of how the failure manifests.

A friend of mine renting an old house had been experiencing his computer shutting down occasionally because it temporarily lost power. This had of course been very frustrating as it meant he would lose work or at least be interrupted from whatever he was working on as he went to flip the breaker. He had been "living with it" for a while, but when he lost some important work he got fed up. As he went for the third time into the kitchen to complain of his computer failing, he realized that he was always complaining to the same roommate—and that the roommate was always heating up leftovers in the microwave. As it happened the house had a very large, powerful microwave, and his room was next to the kitchen.

Once my friend had noticed this pattern, he could quickly deduce the answer to this fairly simple problem: The very large microwave might be tripping the breaker when other appliances (and his desktop computer) were all running at the same time. He tested it and saw the trip happen again. He smiled and grabbed an extension cord to move his computer's supply to his opposite wall. While he and his housemates waited for a less aggressive replacement microwave, he taped over that outlet to make sure he didn't use it by mistake.

## BREAKING DOWN BARRIERS

**Great problem-solvers will overcome barriers to getting the specific information they need.** If a machine is moving too quickly for a problem-solver to see a pattern with their own eyes, a great problem-solver will get a camera to record it, and then slow it down. If a manufacturing line doesn't automatically count units produced, great problem-solvers get out there and do the counting. They work closely with those who best understand the system or process to find where to look to answer each question and find the clearest information.

In a chemical processing plant, some very large (10-ton) pumps were breaking down every 3 months, costing the company tens of millions of dollars per year and posing a safety risk, as containment was lost during failure. The plant had spent years and tens of millions of dollars repeatedly upgrading the pumps to be able to add bigger, harder seals into the pumps to prevent the failures—but they just kept coming.

After yet another failure, a new team had been formed to work on this problem, and it included some members of my team. After the next pump failure occurred, rather than work on even bigger seals back at the desk, we insisted on looking at the pump as it was disassembled in order to better understand what was happening. The team found once again that the seal had been eroded, and there was a smattering of black solid particles all over the seal, mixed into the lubricant. We decided to "smell it" chemically, running it through the lab: The techs there found that the particles were actually an oxidized (or literally "cooked") version of the very chemical that the pumps were pumping. This was a huge insight for the team and set them up to quickly solve this long-thought impossible problem by digging into the fundamentals. You'll see how this problem was solved in Chapter 5, "Dig Into the Fundamentals."

## USING PROBLEM-SMELLING TO BUILD ALIGNMENT

Getting a good pattern of failure can build organizational belief that a problem is solvable. Often hard problems require a commitment of resources and attention from an organization to solve them and implement a solution, and a good pattern can develop buy-in to muster these resources.

One of my favorite examples of this comes from working with a national drink brand that was selling out in stores. The demand for this product was expanding rapidly as the marketing and sales teams had done a phenomenal job. There was huge pressure to increase production to retain as much of the available market share as possible, because copycat products were starting to fill empty shelf space. The organization was planning to build new plants and lines to do this, but it would take 18 months. In the meantime, the existing facilities were working furiously to get everything out the door that they could, and I was brought in to help.

Our analysis turned up a number of opportunities to immediately increase production. The most interesting was to increase the speed of one of the lines. The idea was understandably met with some resistance: Everyone knows that if you run faster you will make more stuff, and the local team knew this, but they also "knew" that the equipment was not capable of going faster. They proved this to me by turning up the speed and creating a huge mess of half-filled bottles flying onto the floor that three of us had to clean up.

I realized that the problem I needed to solve *first* was to give the local team hope and belief that the speed could be successfully increased (I'll talk more about figuring out what problem to work on in Chapter 4, "Know What Problem You're Solving"). Luckily, a conversation with the VP got me permission to work with the operator to test the speed and smell the problem, and we learned a lot. First, we saw that the bottles were kicked off the line due to being underfilled. With careful study I saw that the underfilled bottles came from the same three (of 36) filling heads.

Once the operator and I showed this to the VP, it was clear the problem was solvable, and we got the team on board to move forward. After all, if 33 of the filling heads work then the other three could be made to work as well. Pattern of failure alone had not solved the hard problem of how to get more output from the filler, but it *had* helped me solve the political one of how to get the team on board.

## HOW MUCH IS ENOUGH?

Developing a thorough problem description and pattern of failure is not a matter of gathering reams of data and burying yourself with them. Bad problem solvers in businesses will download long histories of data from points along the entire process or even measure lots of new stuff to try to find something useful. They'll compare every single part between a "good machine" and a "bad" one. These efforts waste a lot of time and money at best, and lead to red herrings in hard problems that mean bad solutions, wasted money, new problems, and a loss of credibility.

Great problem solvers develop the questions that they want to answer before they go about collecting information and data, rather than depending on whatever data streams they see. They grab the signal, not the noise.

But *when* are you done with describing the problem or developing a pattern of failure? In short: never. As you develop insight and dig into the fundamentals, you'll be coming back iteratively to keep smelling: You'll have new understanding to ask new questions. This isn't a step: It's a behavior. Smell the problem to answer questions about it that arise.

If you are a less experienced problem-solver then you will want to practice this rigor on some easier and moderate problems in order to hone the skills you'll need to make rapid progress on harder ones. Some hard problems may only occur once or be very hard to see; being a skilled problem-smeller helps you make decisions when you face these more challenging scenarios.

## NOW: SMELL THE PROBLEM

Get yourself out of your chair and into the field with a notebook. Start gathering information about your problem, and ask the questions in Table 2.1. But most importantly, practice using your powers of observation, with all of your senses, to sift out what is actually happening at the problem. And remember to not distract yourself with solution-guessing!

CHAPTER 3

# Embrace Your Ignorance

*You must unlearn what you have learned.*[1]
—YODA, IN *STAR WARS: EPISODE V—THE EMPIRE STRIKES BACK*

Imagine every movie you've seen in which the main character is out to learn some ancient secret, master a complex martial art, or climb something really tall. They meet their quirky or enigmatic teacher and, after convincing the master to teach them, their training begins. The main character is impatient and tries to achieve the task quickly, using the habits and thinking they have brought from their past. Of course, they fail in some spectacular or hilarious fashion, and the master shakes their head, sighing slowly as they attempt to muster their own patience for their pupil.

Now these stories usually end happily: The martial artist kicks the villain really hard, or the magician levitates the giant thing. Roll credits.

Where did all of these students finally catch traction and enter the happy part of the training montage? The turning point was that they let go of their old thinking and habits. They realized they were on the frontier of understanding, and the assumptions they formed from past experience were detrimental. They embraced their ignorance, and committed themselves to learning what they wished to master by starting from the basics and working up, rather than demonstrating what they believed they knew.

**Great problem-solvers know that they must become masters of the unique problem and the process it affects,**

**and that when they walk into a new situation they must be more focused on learning what they do not yet know than demonstrating the knowledge they already have.** They ask questions others might think are stupid, and challenge what "everyone knows" to make sure they have the facts.

Embracing one's ignorance isn't easy. In many cases we already know 90% of what is required to solve a problem, so it's reasonable to start from a position of knowledge rather than ignorance: People are asking you to solve the problem because of what you know, rather than what you don't. However, it is the last 10% that lies between you and an elegant solution.

## WHY WE HIDE OUR IGNORANCE

Early in my career I would often find myself in a new business that I knew nothing about. Power and respect flowed with experience and tenure, and you were expected to know all the insider language and acronyms. While both experience and shared language serve a purpose to help an organization function well, they can also raise barriers when looking to solve hard problems.

When we were in our first introductory meeting, there might be five or 10 people who would go around a table and say their name, their role, and how long they had worked at the business or in the industry. Mostly they had been in their fields since before I was born. What I learned was that you can't be defensive or try to hide your ignorance. When it was my turn to speak I would always explain that it was my second hour on-site and that I was looking forward to learning more.

Some people, when they hear something they don't understand, ask "What's that?" and they get to learn; others will hold back or nod along because they're worried they're supposed to know what they're hearing—then they're lost. I was reminded of this last week when the acronym "CYOA" was used in a presentation. Well I had no idea what this meant. Was it Cover Your Own Ass? Was it the Caribbean Yacht Owners Association? I asked and it stood for something else—a shame, as for a moment there I thought I was going sailing! In business we are faced with this all the time, and the best problem-solvers simply ask what everything means.

Often we're afraid to admit what we don't know, even to ourselves: It is comforting to imagine that we already have a good idea of the solution to our problem and can take action. This need for comfort is of course reinforced in our upbringings, where we are rewarded for having the right answer now and taking action immediately.

This all raises an interesting question around parenting. Part of your job as a parent is to guide your children, to provide them with basic knowledge, such as:

"Can I drink this?"

"No, it's poison."

Or:

"Is it okay to run around with this toilet brush?"

"I think it's best not to."

And kids are great believers in their parents. But where do you draw the line between giving them your best guess of how something works and helping them gain knowledge, and making it *appear* like one always has an answer to something, rather than admitting we don't know and looking something up? Fortunately, smartphones and the ability to check something out on Wikipedia means it's easier than ever to demonstrate searching for knowledge rather than retaining data in your head.

And asking questions can also be emotionally difficult. People are afraid to look stupid in front of peers and friends, colleagues, and clients. Imagine you're at a party and someone you've met calls your name as they approach you from the table of snacks. "Nat! So good to see you again!" For a quarter-second, you freeze. *Uh oh: I don't know this guy's name.* But you play it cool. "Hey! How's the..." You check his ring finger, and there's a wedding band. Excellent. "Family?" He smiles, grateful that you're thinking about him, and tells you all the great stuff his kids are up to. You sigh in relief: bullet dodged. Now you just have to wait for someone to say his name, and *this* time you'll remember.

I've done this before, because I've just been too embarrassed to say, "Oh gosh can you remind me of your name?" And I know the longer that I pretend to know and don't just ask the guy (or someone else) his name, the more I'm going to look like a complete buffoon if I get into a situation where someone's expecting a name and I can't provide it. Take the hit to your pride and solve the problem.

Ultimately, it is fear of being "exposed" that causes many people to hide behind their ignorance and accept poor problem-solving. There's a fear of public failure when you commit yourself or your resources to solving a hard problem. Even when diving into a problem, there's a fear of looking ignorant or "stupid" by asking questions one is "supposed to know."

## WHAT HAPPENS WHEN WE HIDE BEHIND IGNORANCE

Just as was the case for me at that party, many nascent problem-solvers will run away from or cope with their ignorance of a problem. I've seen smart people run away from problems in logistics, IT, sales growth, and safety by immediately calling in and passing the buck to subject matter experts because the would-be problem-solvers are afraid of their ignorance—more on this in Chapter 6, "Don't Rely on Experts."

I remember working with a business that made and packaged food for grocery stores. At the end of a production line the product was put into cardboard boxes for shipping and then carried on down the line to be sealed up and stacked on a pallet. They had an automatic box-closing machine to seal the cases, but I noticed someone standing at the conveyor just before it all day, prefolding the flaps of the boxes, because sometimes the automatic box closer did not work. I nicknamed this position the "box-blesser."

What's wrong with this solution? Well, it obviously takes someone away from doing more useful work. And imagine how boring that job must be. The box-closing machine had some trouble a few years earlier, and it made sense to put someone in that role temporarily to make sure the production line ran that day. But everyone had run away from the fact that they did not understand how to make the automatic box-closing machine work again, so the box-blesser became a permanent position.

I was in the fortunate position of being naturally ignorant, and when I arrived, the person prefolding the box flaps seemed odd to me. I embraced my ignorance and asked, "Why is that person there?" When it was explained to me, I asked, "What happens when we run boxes through without the prefolding?" Nobody was sure, so we tried it, and learned a lot about the problem by watching it occur.

I noticed that many of the boxes went through and were sealed without any issue. I was also able to figure out where in the machine the jams did occur, and therefore saw quickly what changes needed to happen to allow the machine to work well every time. The first step to solving this problem came from embracing and running towards what we didn't know.

Another business was having trouble retaining high-level management positions, and just kept increasing salaries and benefits in the hopes that they would keep good people, when the underlying root cause was the sense of autonomy and meaning these people found in the work. Nobody wanted to ask them why they were leaving; perhaps it was uncomfortable. But as soon as the exit interviews were changed, they found the root cause and were able to get started fixing it. But for years, the HR department was afraid to approach the problem from a position of "fresh eyes" ignorance and ended up losing great talent because of it.

Next is one of my favorite company myth stories, and it involves "dinosaur hair." A large industrial facility in the energy industry had a process step that required product to be forced through small nozzles to purify it. Apparently, production was limited because the nozzles clogged up with dinosaur hair that was in the material when the oil was formed. I don't know how the dinosaur hair was supposed to have survived the geological processes required to make oil or whether dinosaurs even had hair, but I do know that the financial impact of these clogs was very large.

This legend served an important function in the business. It freed people from having to figure out a solution to the problem. In some ways it was a solution to the political side of the clogged nozzle problem: it subtly rebranded the problem from "clogged nozzles" to "dinosaur hair." After all, does anyone have a solution for dinosaur hair? It would need to be something unlikely, such as borrowing a Tardis from Dr. Who and a large razor from Conan the Barbarian.

How do you make progress in these situations? After all this oil production facility was a huge place filled with very competent staff who had plenty of advanced degrees in things few people understand about the petrochemical industry. But far from being unusual, this is a very common situation in all walks of life. People are socialized not to "challenge" what respected people believe.

What stories exist in your life that prevent you from approaching your fear of the unknown?

## EMBRACE YOUR IGNORANCE, THEN SLAY IT

**A great problem-solver will gently challenge the organization rather than individuals, and have the humility to lead by example, by demonstrating their ignorance.**

Imagine this scenario:

"What is this material?"

"Dinosaur hair."

"Have we chemically analyzed it to determine what it is?"

"Well, no."

As I'm sure I foreshadowed with a bit of a heavy hand, the clogging material was not dinosaur hair. It was, in fact, a man-made fiber being mistakenly introduced into the process at the facility. Smashing the "dinosaur hair" myth by embracing ignorance got this excellent team on track to rapidly solve the problem.

Moving towards the true cause of a problem is going to require fresh eyes that want to learn. This is why outside problem-solvers sometimes have an advantage with hard problems over those familiar with the system: A common cognitive bias is the "curse of knowledge," where our brains assume that the problem we're looking at is similar to something we've seen in the past.

**Great problem-solvers aren't afraid of their ignorance, and they're not afraid of others seeing it.** Great questions shatter assumptions, provoke new insight, and position those that do know about the process or system to contribute their expertise. Great problem-solvers build confidence and don't need to position themselves as all-knowing (see Table 3.1). They know that nobody is all-knowing about any process, and this is particularly true of something highly complex. Nobody alone knows enough about an F-22 Raptor or the global financial system to solve its many problems without asking some great questions.

| Table 3.1: Remember, you're not supposed to know everything. |
| --- |
| There are over 16 million books and 120 million other items in the Library of Congress. |
| There are over 6 million parts in a Boeing 747. |
| The US Tax Code is over 4 million words in length. |
| There are over 1 billion websites in the world. |

I remember when I was 19 at an internship in Los Angeles. One of the guys there, Dr. Mack Quan, gave me a lot of good advice, but one story he told really stuck in my head. "When you've received your bachelor's degree, you think you know everything. Once you get your master's, you realize you don't know anything. When you get your PhD, you realize nobody really knows anything." This is a great story to remember when approaching novel problems. For some reason, realizing that no one else really knows a lot about things helps me jump in with both feet.

**But great problem-solvers don't just admit their ignorance. They *embrace* it.** They understand that introducing a little bit of smart ignorance into a problem-solving effort will get people asking questions for which they assumed they already had answers. Great problem solvers use their ignorance to help experts close to the problem or process to explain their understanding thoroughly, and in that explanation sort out fact from assumption. Often, the effort of merely explaining a complex process to a smart, ignorant person actually causes the people closest to the problem to develop new understanding and insight.

Once in the late '90s I found myself working in a factory that made toothpaste tubes that went to other factories for filling, and they weren't able to meet customer demand. They made these tubes by forming a cylinder, chopping it to length, and then welding on the threaded top using induction welding. When they ran the machine near its rated speed, the welds would burn the tubes, and they had to be thrown out. Running slower made the quality problem go away, but then they couldn't produce enough.

I had some theoretical knowledge of induction from college, but no idea how it worked in practice. I asked a lot of questions of the operators, mechanics, and managers. They explained that when they slowed the machine, they could turn down the power of the induction welder, so it wouldn't burn. I didn't understand it all, so I read the manual at the hotel overnight. I can't remember the technical details now, but a section on the "shape of the waveform" taught me what I needed: It just required embracing my ignorance and hunting out the answers. I shared this section with the operators and mechanics, and we were able to go faster by significantly increasing the power of the welder, but for a shorter period of time so there was no time to burn: the opposite of the strategy previously applied.

The mechanics ultimately didn't understand how the welder worked, but they were afraid to admit their ignorance to themselves or others. They probably had not picked up the manual in a long time, but the key insight to understand what needed to change was right there.

Being willing to expose your ignorance can be hard, until you learn the costs of not doing so.

## DO YOU KNOW HOW TO BUILD A DECK?

A number of years ago we decided to build a deck off the back of our home, so I dutifully purchased a "how to build a deck" book. My wife figured I might need a little more practical understanding, so she signed me up for a two-session deck-building school at Home Depot. I am sure it was not because she was nervous!

I like these opportunities to explore new skills and was not afraid to get stuck in and learn how to practically apply my largely theoretical knowledge. I was the only engineer in the course and most of my peers thought it was a joke that I was taking it. Of course, as an engineer I should be able to figure this out on my own, right? But I doubt any of them knew how to build a deck, and of course many would not want to admit this.

As it happens, I learned a lot about deck building and it was especially useful for the more tricky parts, such as cutting stringers for the stairs. I "passed" the course and even got a merit badge— like boy scouts get for demonstrating a skill. It was great fun and super fulfilling. I went on to build more decks and help friends put them in. You can do a lot when you're willing to admit you don't really understand something. Having a spouse who can help you understand these gaps is also helpful!

## NOW: EMBRACE YOUR IGNORANCE

Go and look up something that you don't really understand as well as you would like. Something you bluff your way through. It might be how the clutch works on a manual car or which country has the third largest population.

Also, next time someone mentions something and you don't know what it is, stop and ask them. In fact, do that even if you are certain you do know. Practice feeling comfortable acquiring knowledge.

CHAPTER 4

# Know What Problem You're Solving

*A problem well-stated is a problem half-solved.*[1]
—CHARLES KETTERING, AMERICAN ENGINEER,
HOLDER OF 186 PATENTS, INVENTOR OF THE ELECTRICAL
STARTING MOTOR, LEADED GASOLINE, AND FREON REFRIGERANT

Extreme poverty is one of the globe's most important and damaging problems. As a society we have made great progress: In 1990, 37% of the world's population (or 1.95 billion people) lived on less than $1.90 per day. By 2012, that number dropped to 12.7%, representing 900 million people lifted from poverty using this definition. That's an incredible change, but there are still almost a billion people living in extreme poverty. And while the modern economy has been a miracle to many regions, such as East Asia and South America, places like sub-Saharan Africa have been largely left behind: 42.6% of people there remain in extreme poverty.

Between individual donors, nongovernmental organizations (NGOs), national governments, and the United Nations, hundreds of billions of dollars have been thrown at sub-Saharan Africa to alleviate poverty through massive infrastructure projects, donations of food or goods, or underpriced loans. But poverty has remained stubborn, and some believe that these aid programs have actually backfired and suppressed growth in high-poverty areas.

Paul Polak started a group called International Development Enterprises, which has brought 17 million people out of poverty by improving their productivity. He believes that those large-scale

51

programs have failed because they were working on the wrong problems. In his book, *Out of Poverty,* he calls the approaches based on projects, loans, and donations "The Great Poverty Eradication Myths," and demonstrates quite decisively that they have all failed.[2]

Polak's approach to poverty reduction is an example of really incredible problem-solving, and his organization demonstrates many of the behaviors of great problem-solvers. One great example from his book is how he smelled the problem so thoroughly. Instead of attempting to determine from a conference room in New York what solutions poor families needed, Polak has invested the vast majority of his time up-front in smell mode. Polak himself has "talked with over 3,000 poor families," and "walked with them through their fields" to understand what life was like for them on the ground.[3] He understood end-to-end how they acquired seed stock, planted it, cultivated it, harvested it, and brought it to market, in each specific area. He learned the market pressures that each region faced, individually.

Doing this helped him to make a radical breakthrough in understanding the problem itself: **The amount and type of crops they produce does not provide enough value for them to escape poverty.** By accurately defining the problem of poverty as low labor productivity, Polak was able to focus on improving lives by solving the specific root causes of that low labor productivity in different regions. He had found that most of his clients were one-acre farmers that grew low yields of cheap crops during peak season. To increase the value of their labor, he found that, in each specific market, his clients could instead grow higher yields of higher-value crops in the off-season, where the prices are higher. To do this, they needed a steady supply of more water, so he produced simple irrigation systems powered by foot-driven treadle pumps to supply that water.

It was Polak's years of smelling the problem, on site, with the families he was trying to help, that enabled him to define the problem correctly and solve it with a cheap, elegant solution that has lifted millions out of poverty.

That's the difference between knowing what problem you're working on, and not. Perhaps many aid organizations make assumptions about the problem they are solving, and throw hundreds of billions of dollars at the problem to little or no effect. Polak, by defining the problem correctly, has created an effective, permanent, and self-funding process that continues to bring people out of poverty.

Successfully solving hard problems requires knowing what problem you're solving. **You should put great care into defining the problem in an accurate and precise way, as a direct and measurable observation of the problem.** It must be clear how solving it translates directly to your goals. And it must *absolutely not* be an assumption or jump-to-conclusion.

## THE DANGER OF BAD PROBLEM DEFINITIONS

A bad problem definition is a particularly insidious form of guessing. When a "problem definition" is an assumption about the solution, it puts blinders on the problem-solver's eyes, and they gallop straight toward the entirely wrong cause with unjustified confidence. This leads to investing resources—our time, money, emotional energy—into something that won't solve our problem at all, or might make it worse.

You may have observed some bad problem definitions in your business or your life. You might have an asset that starts to break or put out bad product at high speeds, and the operators may say that the problem is that "the machine is running too fast." That's not a problem: A problem is what's happening *when it runs too fast,* and that's a problem that you can solve. The only way to solve "it's too fast" is to slow it down, and that prohibits solving the problem at all.

| Table 4.1: Problem assumptions vs. problem definitions. | |
| --- | --- |
| Problem Assumption | Problem Definition |
| "The pump is broken." | "The pressure from the pump is too low." |
| "We have too many semiautomatic weapons." | "Premature/wrongful death is too high." |
| "Not enough people own handguns to protect themselves." | "Premature/wrongful death is too high." |
| "The toilet is too old." | "The toilet is leaking water." |
| "I must have a low metabolic rate." | "I am unhappy with my weight." |
| "My spouse must be tired and grumpy." | "Right now I do not feel emotionally close to my spouse." |

This happens all the time in problems of personal conflict, too. How many times have you heard two people declare that the other one is a jerk, or otherwise badly intentioned? You can't solve the problem of your colleague or family member being a terrible person. You *can* solve a problem that involves a misunderstanding, miscommunication, or misalignment.

Great problem-solvers avoid being trapped into solving the wrong problem by defining the problem without prejudice or assumption (see Table 4.1). They define the problem that they see, and in the scope of the measurable or tangible thing that they want. Consider our case of "dinosaur hair": what the organization *wanted* was nozzles that didn't clog, so the nozzle clogging was the problem. By calling it a "dinosaur hair" problem, the company got stuck with a seemingly unsolvable situation that didn't exist at all.

It's probable that you and others around you are misdefining problems all the time, and it keeps you from even beginning to solve them. Great problem-solvers keep checking whether they have defined the problem incorrectly by letting assumptions or prejudices creep in.

## DEFINING THE PROBLEM AS A VARIABLE

Perhaps the most useful approach for defining the problem well is structuring it as a measurable variable. With this, we view the problem as something we can measure objectively, and we remove the guessed solution and a lot of emotion. We know that we have a problem when this variable is not in the range we want (that is, "out of spec"), and we don't have a problem once it's brought into a range that's acceptable ("in spec").

Defining the problem as a variable helps us be specific about what the problem really is. If we have insufficient pressure in our shower head, defining the problem as "low water pressure" rather than "a broken shower" immediately sets us on a more helpful path to solving it. Same goes for, "our accountant turnover rate is too high," rather than "we have an HR problem." A "low in-full on-time percentage" is a better problem definition than "our distribution network is a mess." Defining the acceptable and unacceptable ranges for this variable means that the problem definition is objective and immune to opinion.

Without a measurable variable, we might end up taking the wrong approach, even if we're not guessing. Your friends say they want to be in better shape, but that means different things to different people. One might want to lose weight by reducing body mass, another increase strength by increasing muscle mass, and another increase endurance for a long distance race. You would measure these with different variables, and approach these problems differently.

In some less technical problems, you may not be able to measure the primary variable with as much rigor. For instance, perhaps your problem is "I am too angry in X situations," and you'll need to use your judgment to measure anger in a consistent way. So perhaps you just write in a notebook how angry you feel, on a 1 to 10 scale. Developing the skill to do this takes time, but once the behavior is ingrained it will be second nature.

This is like Goldilocks: There's a porridge that's too hot and too cold, and we want the one that's just right.

## GETTING A GREAT PROBLEM DEFINITION

In the end, even with a measurable variable at hand, the problem-solver will use the context around them to determine the right way to define the problem they're working on. Doing this poorly will be frustrating, but doing it well will usually accelerate the team toward quicker victory. As you develop your skills, having a strong problem-solving method to guide you in problem definition will be very helpful. I've got some guidance for you to choose a helpful approach in Chapter 10, "How to Choose Your Method." You may even find that you redefine the problem as you smell it out more. This is fine.

I've found that getting a well-defined, measured problem definition can help people understand where a problem exists when they were previously blind to it. Let's take a look at an issue that many parents encounter: Kids often spend too much time on their electronics. This can end up as a debate that goes a bit like this:

"You're spending too much time on electronics."

"YOU DON'T UNDERSTAND ME, DAD!"

Angry stalemate ensues.

This topic came up recently with my eldest son. I've gotten to know my son fairly well in the time I've been his dad, and I realized that arguing back and forth about how much time was right to spend on electronics was not going to be productive. He's a smart guy, and coming to him to say, "You're doing too much of X" without any data wasn't going to cut it, so I tried another tack.

One day I asked him if he had a personal target for how much time he wanted to spend on electronics per week, because the first level of this problem was that we weren't aligned on such a target. You can imagine this approach was better received. He thought about it for a bit and gave me a number. I thought this was a little high, but was a step in the right direction, so that problem was quickly solved. We now had a new problem that we were both aligned on—"We don't know how much time he was using electronics per week"—so we had to measure it.

I suggested he start logging his electronics time so we could see how he was doing versus his target. He came up with the great idea to simply look at the data in his Steam gaming account. He was shocked with what he found, as he was spending far more hours a week gaming than he thought was reasonable. It turns out that a 5-minute traffic jam can feel like an hour and an afternoon on the computer can seem like 10 minutes. Then we were both aligned on the "too much time" problem, which is critical, as he was in the best position to fix it. My son is smart, motivated, and not much interested in self-deception. When he got to grips with this issue, he set a plan in motion to change things. Better understanding of the problem that needed to be solved, and then simply measuring the current state, were enough to help in many ways, including enhancing my relationship with my teenage son!

So how do you know for certain that you have the right problem definition? Ultimately, there's no recipe for this: It requires skill that you need to develop by practicing this behavior. As we've seen in some examples above, sometimes you may miss the mark and have to shift.

Sometimes you'll get it wrong, and that's fine. This is a behavior you're using constantly, so at some point when really smelling the problem you're going to find that you misdefined the problem, and that's a moment where you've made progress. You learned, and that puts you a step closer. You'll get better at this with practice. But there are two critical pitfalls to avoid in this process: leaving your scope and making assumptions during the problem definition.

## KEEPING IN YOUR SCOPE

I've frequently seen teams define problems as too broad or out of their scope. Doing so will confuse the problem-solver or team, and cause delays in one of three ways:

- They consider and study a range of variables that is too wide

- They work on problems that are outside of their power, skills, or authority

- They're actually running away from the problem in some way

Let us consider almost any problem in a publicly owned business. Ultimately, the goal of the business is some form of socially responsible return to its shareholders. If your team is trying to reduce the business's carbon footprint, the problem definition for the team is the business's carbon footprint, *not* global warming. This is a fairly obvious example, but defining the problem properly keeps the team from wandering into purely academic discussions about the business possibly investing in electric cars or solar power. Similarly, a team tasked with improving supply-chain logistics shouldn't focus on "business profit," because it could begin similarly distracting discussions about marketing strategy.

Looking outside of our scope can be a way of running away from a problem. Subconsciously, a problem-solver or team may want to take the heat off themselves, and may point to another business unit that is underperforming, and say, "we should really be focusing there!"

When the price of oil dropped in 2015, I remember many of our petrochemical clients saying that their problem was that the price of oil was low. This is a great example of a problem definition that is too high in the clouds: What could they do to affect it? Go to OPEC meetings and make a persuasive speech? Start an international incident that cuts off the Strait of Hormuz? This is all possible in Hollywood but not practical elsewhere.

A better problem definition is one in the problem-solver's wheelhouse: They had the ability to control their operating costs. They could all reduce their marginal cost per barrel, reduce their overhead, and improve the value of their capital projects—and focusing there is the only way they could have reliably reduced the pain they and their shareholders felt. As some of my Canadian friends have told me: "There is no such thing as bad weather; just the wrong clothes." This is particularly important in a commodity business: The slowest impala in the herd is the one that gets eaten, and you can't run fast when you are busy thinking about things you can't impact.

Great problem-solvers avoid this by defining the problem as something that's in their sphere of influence. They understand the context of the problem and how solving it relates directly to those higher-level goals of the business by engaging leadership and those close to the problem and financials.

## AVOIDING ASSUMPTIONS

One of the most dangerous—and most pervasive—mistakes when creating a problem definition is letting some assumption about the key drivers sneak in before really understanding the full scope of the problem.

I've seen a lot of asset-reliability problems in my time, in which some critical piece of equipment breaks down, and the downtime costs productivity. It could be a conveyor or a computer. I've frequently seen the maintenance or IT department focusing on improving response time. So they'll work on improving their ticketing system, or creating a cart for tools, rather than focusing on overall downtime of the asset and solving the problem that's making the thing break in the first place. This broad approach can drive some results, though it requires a significant change effort that often erodes with time. However, by looking at it in a one-dimensional way the root cause of the downtime is frequently ignored. Fix the problem!

Many years ago as a young consultant, when I had a little less problem-solving experience, I was working with a food packaging company that made nutritional bars. They were facing an operating loss each quarter, spending more money than they made. The customer liked the product so this business could sell more if they could make it. We were tasked with increasing throughput using the existing assets to meet customer demand. We found the plant bottleneck and were able to greatly increase its output by solving a number of neat problems.

When the monthly results came back, we were a little surprised to see that the plant financials were worse against budget than the month before. This was strange, since the extra production shipped should have improved profit by quite a bit.

We spent a few hours digging through the profit and loss (P&L) details with the plant staff and realized after a while that the business's total marginal costs were higher than their marginal revenues: They were losing money on every bar they made. The more we made, the more money was drained—something I had not appreciated when we got going on the production problem.

Some further investigation showed that the facility was making the bars overweight. Had we taken the time to learn this before getting to work, we would have worked on this problem first, and been profitable the last quarter. We had worked on the wrong problem, based on a baked-in assumption. Let me tell you, this was painful and a lesson I have taken to heart: Always check that you are operating at the right level and get the facts to confirm that, even when you are not invited to do so!

## NOW: KNOW WHAT PROBLEM YOU'RE SOLVING

It's time to go back to the problem you're working on and make sure you really know what it is. Clear your mind of prejudices and assumptions, and look to define the problem as something you can objectively measure to determine whether the problem is happening or not.

Ask yourself these questions when considering your problem definition:

- Is it defined as a measurable variable?

- Does it clearly translate to your higher-level goals?

- Is it within your sphere of influence, or are you overreaching and need help?

- Does your definition include any assumptions about what is causing the problem?

**CHAPTER 5**

# Dig Into the Fundamentals

*If you can't explain it simply, you don't understand it well
enough.*

—ALBERT EINSTEIN, PHYSICIST

Do you know how your toilet works? When you lift the lid off
the tank and look inside, what are all the parts in there meant to
do? Why does water sit in the bowl, rather than just drain away?
There's a lot of stuff people don't understand about toilets, even
though most of us use one every day. The same is true for many
other things all around us: the gearbox in your car, the speaker
in your phone, or how your onions get caramelized on the grill.

There are so many systems and processes in the world that
you can't know how they all work. It would be beyond anyone's
capability, and be a waste of your time. The interesting thing is
when there's a problem with a system that you interact with, you
have three options to attempt to solve it: You can rely on your
superficial knowledge of the system, you can rely on an expert,
or you can dig into the fundamentals. This means learning how
things work at a basic level so you can build up the understanding
you need to truly solve the problem. If you want to solve hard
problems you are going to have to dig in and learn for yourself.

So let's say your toilet had a problem. Don't be intimidated!
This is very old stuff, made of incredibly simple technology, and
anyone reading this book can understand it. With 10 minutes of

research, you can learn a few things. The reason the modern toilet works is due to the siphoning effect, which is the same process someone uses to get stale fuel out of a car tank, or that you use to drain your kids' paddling pool. You'll learn about the different basic types of toilet, and what all the parts do, with handy animations. Same goes for your gearbox, your speaker, and your onion. It's easy to learn about this stuff, but most people don't bother.

I don't suggest you burn your time learning about all of these right now. But next time you have a leak from the tank into your toilet bowl, where you hear it slowly refilling, go find out how it works! Give it a go! If you do this, you might be able to get a $1.79 flapper from the hardware store, and watch a 2-minute video online to learn how to replace it...or, you can call a plumber, wait a week, and pay $150 for the same result. For fairly easy problems, not digging into the fundamentals might cost you a few hundred bucks. For hard problems, really important ones, it can cost your business millions. Personally, it can cost you time, relationships, and quality of life.

When a system isn't working right, someone has to understand how it's meant to work, at the right depth, in order to fix it. Your job as a problem-solver is to dig deep enough into the fundamentals of the specific parts of the system that affect the problem so you can solve it in a methodical, step-by-step way. This is true for machines, mortgage processing systems, and our brains. So whether it's your toilet, your inventory system, or your achy left shoulder, understanding the fundamentals behind it is going to help you. For solving *hard* problems, it's a critical factor to success.

I recall a colleague of mine working at a chemical processing facility that was filled with sensors to measure pressure, flow, temperature, and other variables in the process. Part of the sensors function was to send an alarm to operators if any of these variables reached unsafe levels. There were thousands of these sensors throughout the plant, and hundreds of them were going off as "false positives" every day. Operators would constantly override them, knowing they were broken, but this posed a significant safety risk: What if the pressure in a valve *had* become too high?

This colleague brought a fresh approach to solving the problem: He dug into the scientific fundamentals of how the sensors turned physical inputs into electrical signals, and then into the programming of how the computers turned the incoming electrical signals into alarms. By doing this, he found that a few sensors were malfunctioning and causing almost all of the alarms. When the engineers knew specifically what few sensors were malfunctioning, they were able to quickly and cheaply replace them and create housings that would preserve the integrity of their electrical signals, and tweak computer programming to accurately respond to signals that represented safety or danger.

Digging into the fundamentals has been at the root of some of the most important problem-solving in modern society. Back in the early 1900s, the United States had a major dental hygiene problem: Most people didn't brush their teeth even though they already knew it was important, and so folks lost teeth, got gum disease, and were just generally pretty gross.

An advertising genius named Claude C. Hopkins was tasked to solve this problem (and help an old friend make some serious money) by getting people to use a new toothpaste called Pepsodent. Lots of folks had tried to advertise toothpaste before, but to little avail.

Hopkins, though, had dug into the fundamentals of psychology. It was the early days of modern psychology, so he couldn't just look in a textbook. But he had learned that in order to get people to use something every day, it had to become a habit. And he knew from his experience that the best way to build habits was to establish a clear link between a cue, a routine, and a reward.

To find his cue, he read a whole bunch of dry dental textbooks, but found that plaque built up on your teeth over time. He knew he was on to something: his advertising cued people to use their tongue to feel the plaque on their teeth (cue), get rid of it with a quick brush with Pepsodent (routine), and then enjoy the clean, tingly feeling (reward). In short, it worked brilliantly, toothbrushing quickly became a national habit, Hopkins made millions, and America's dental hygiene problem was largely solved. Hopkins's understanding of habitual psychology was so good that modern psychiatrists, advertisers, and public policy designers still use that same habit loop today. If you'd like to read more about this case, it's in Charles Duhigg's *The Power of Habit.*[1]

## UNDERSTANDING WHAT CONTROLS THE PRIMARY VARIABLE

For a hard problem in a complex system, you're going to get quickly overwhelmed if you try to dig into everything at once. The human body is a great example of this. Another is a computer network that has tens of thousands of nodes of many types. And I can only imagine the complexity of a nuclear power station.

A great problem-solver won't attempt to learn everything: To do so will waste tremendous time without making progress. Spending a few weeks or months learning about an entire system before getting to work is a great way to hide and avoid the challenge of actually solving the problem. Instead, they'll dig into what's *relevant*. The relevant parts of the system are those that impact the primary variable (such as "low water pressure") as discussed in Chapter 4, "Know What Problem You're Solving." You want to understand the fundamentals of the small portion of the system that directly controls your primary variable, rather than trying to understand the whole thing.

When I finished working on the toothpaste tube machine I described in Chapter 3, "Embrace Your Ignorance," I knew as much as anyone about the three or four parts of the system that needed to change so we could increase production, centered around the spot welder. I didn't know a thing about the other 96% of the machine because it wasn't relevant: I'm not an expert on a toothpaste tube machine and never will be. The point was to learn a lot about the part of the system that affects the problem.

But I know a thing or two about solving problems, and I know how to get the specific information that I need in order to understand and solve the problem, either from reading a book, reviewing first principles, or working with people close to the system to learn the science, the function, and what it all looks like. Some people might be interested in learning how the whole thing works, but I'm interested in solving hard problems, and there's no shortage of those! I want to learn what's strictly necessary, solve the problem, and move on.

## WHAT GOOD DIGGING LOOKS LIKE

Let's say you've got a problem with your lawn. The grass is too long, so you'll define your primary variable as length of grass. You want to understand what controls the length of the grass. When I ask people this question in a problem-solving workshop, they'll typically give me a dozen perfectly valid variables that influence the length of the grass. The list might look something like this:

- Rain

- Water drainage

- Nitrates in the soil

- Temperature

- Humidity

- Worms in soil

- Destructive bugs

- Goats that eat the grass

- Weeds per square foot

- How often people walk on the grass

- Species of grass

- Height of your lawn mower blade

And all sorts of other stuff. The smarter and larger the group is, and the more time we put in, the longer a list we get—and this is just your lawn! Imagine trying to check and measure all of these variables. You may have noticed that when it's approached this way, it looks suspiciously like brainstorming—and you know how I feel about that. Imagine something far more complex: To have any hope, we need to simplify this picture. **We need to understand what variables most directly control our primary variable by understanding the science behind how the system works.** Let's look at Figure 5.1 to illustrate this.

**Figure 5.1: Variables controlling the length of your grass**

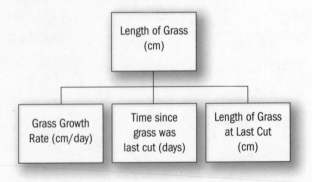

These three variables are the highest-level variables that control the length of the grass: grass growth rate, time since grass was last cut, and length of grass at last cut. Focusing on them, you can methodically break down what you need to understand in a way you can get your arms around. We know these grass variables are complete and correct because the math works out: If you multiply rate and time, then add that to the length at the last cut, you know you have the current height of the grass. Digging into the fundamentals in this very precise way helps us understand exactly and specifically what controls our problem.

If instead you run off a list of 20 different factors that control the height of the grass, you're bound to miss something, and you're going to run around measuring 20 things, all of which exist as subvariables to these highest-level variables.

Once we have the highest-level variables, we can expand out to the next level in a similar way when this is needed to help solve the problem. But you don't want to waste a lot of time doing it when it's not necessary, as it just adds complexity. The lawn example is fairly trivial, but you can see that for something with hundreds of muscles and bones, or thousands of pipes and wires, you'll want to do this in a controlled way. This is about simplifying, rather than adding complexity. We'll pick up more on this in Chapter 9, "Stay on Target."

## FURTHER BENEFITS OF DIGGING IN

**Approaching problems in this way turns a potentially sprawling problem with a thousand dead ends into something you can get your arms around, making steady progress.** For hard problems, this level of rigor is necessary to win, but it even has benefits for somewhat simpler problems:

- It will reduce the amount of testing and measurement required.

- It will save you time.

- Your understanding of the critical elements of the process or system will be better by the end, often allowing you to optimize further in the future.

- It allows you to create simpler management systems and more effectively train your staff.

- You will have built a clear, compelling story supporting the solution, allowing you to build consensus around implementation.

- You ingrain the key behaviors that will allow you to solve hard problems.

The pump seal problem in the chemical processing facility simply couldn't have been solved without digging into the fundamentals. Recall that in Chapter 2, "Smell the Problem," we found that we had oxidized chemical product where it shouldn't be. Knowing about oxidization and heat transfer taught us that the temperature at the seal was too high, so the lubricating coolant for the seal (the "seal flush") must not be doing its job.

We measured the flow of the seal flush and learned that it was far too low despite the pressure being on-spec; using Bernoulli's principle we eliminated every high-level variable except the cross-sectional area of the pipe.[2] Knowing with certainty that the cross-sectional area was too small, we were able to confidently search for a blockage in the pipe that happened to be 50 feet. Nobody had guessed this, and it's unlikely anyone would have. Solving hard problems can require learning or refreshing some complex stuff. You may have forgotten some of the science so you'll be learning something brand new. But you can't shy away: If you want to solve these problems, you'll need to embrace your ignorance and dig in!

To dig into the fundamentals, you'll need to learn both the particulars of that system, and some of the science behind it. Sometimes you'll need to break out the manual or textbook, go online, and get support from someone who knows more about whatever you're working on than you do.

## WHY PATTERN OF FAILURE ALONE IS INSUFFICIENT

We considered in Chapters 2 and 4, "Smell the Problem" and "Know What Problem You're Solving," that with simple problems and a strong problem definition, you can sometimes solve problems by finding the pattern of failure. This can be a valid approach to start with, but with hard problems it is unlikely to resolve the issue. There are a few specific ways that pattern-finding, while important, falls short in solving hard problems.

First, **correlation is not causation**. Just because two things happen simultaneously does not mean that one causes the other. There's a reason this is a tired adage. There are going to be lots of variables with correlations between them in hard problems. Failing to understand the fundamentals means you have no way of knowing what correlation is pointing to cause, and what is a coincidence or red herring.

In most cases, you simply have no idea where to look for the right data without knowing the fundamentals. If you've got a very complex system, whether it's a natural or a man-made process, you may have hundreds of signals coming off of it, all of which can be turned into data. If you don't know the fundamentals, you're flying blind and will bury yourself.

Second, sometimes **you can't see what's going on**. I call this the "it's dark down there" problem. When my team was helping with an unproductive oil well hundreds of feet below the surface, there was precious little data about the conditions in the well. They solved the problem by mastering the well map and studying the geological science.

Third, sometimes t**he problem is unique or only happened once**. In these cases, problem-solving that relies on pattern-finding is of no use at all. If we look at the Challenger space shuttle catastrophe, there weren't any patterns to be found, period. It happened once.

Finally, **the variable you need to fix may not change, so it doesn't create a pattern**. I was working with a food company that had recently gone through a large sourcing project to reduce the cost of their cardboard boxes by millions of dollars. One day, the team was complaining that ever since they had switched to the cheaper cardboard boxes, they had problems with their case erector, which takes a flat box and turns it into a cube.

They'd been beating up their box supplier, telling them to improve quality, and were expending a lot of energy complaining about the purchasing effort that had saved their plant a few hundred thousand dollars in materials, but was costing them production in jamming. Pattern of failure suggested they should switch back to the old box supplier, saving them the aggravation but costing them savings from the purchasing project.

In reality, when we dug into the fundamentals and learned what affected the shape of the boxes coming out of the case erector, we identified a few out-of-control, but unchanging, variables on the erector. When we corrected them, the plant could run all of the boxes from all suppliers. If this sounds similar to the box-blesser problem from Chapter 3, "Embrace Your Ignorance," don't think you are crazy. People fail to dig into how things work all the time. I've seen the outcome of this destructive pattern of behavior more times than I care to think about: A business damages its relationship with its supplier because it's not solving its own problems well.

## DIGGING INTO THE FUNDAMENTALS OF OUR EVERYDAY LIVES

The negative consequences of trying to solve hard problems using only pattern of failure are littered throughout our lives. I remember when I was younger going out to breakfast with my uncle when we were visiting him while on vacation from Hong Kong where I grew up. My uncle had been diagnosed with high cholesterol, so he was told to avoid eggs. At breakfast one day, my dad ordered a fairly elaborate three-egg omelet. The look on my uncle's face is burned into my mind. He gazed longingly at my dad's plate and said, "I'm only allowed one egg per week." He really liked his eggs.

In the hopes of limiting the buildup of cholesterol in the body, doctors used to advise people to minimize their cholesterol intake. If you had high cholesterol, you were told that you should avoid it almost completely.

But back then most people didn't understand the fundamentals—that the body breaks down the cholesterol it ingests into constituent parts, and our body makes its own cholesterol, and there are ways to control that. How much cholesterol you eat is probably almost irrelevant to your blood cholesterol.

This is bad problem-solving. Doctors were well intentioned, but their advice was just their best guess. They had a correlation and a good story to go with it, and they've driven people to eat things that were probably less healthy than the eggs they were banning.

This is one of the reasons why I'm so passionate about this, and so frustrated with bad problem-solving: There's not just an economic impact from bad problem-solving. There's a very deep human one, too. Good problem-solving in our lives leads to greater happiness, health, and flourishing, and I want the world to be full of better problem-solvers that can bring this about.

Understanding the fundamentals of metabolism, hunger, and psychology can help with problems as seemingly elusive as weight loss. This is a huge problem in the United States and something that a lot of people struggle with and suffer from. Many people try very hard to lose weight and fail.

If you've smelled the problem, you may have perhaps learned that you eat more calories than you should (if you haven't, I recommend tracking for a few days how many calories you're taking in—this is critical for your problem description). As you dig into what controls how much you eat, you'll of course find that hunger is one of the variables. Perhaps in the past you've just tried to eat less, but failed because you get hungry.

The medical community has made great advancements in recent years understanding how different foods affect us, and some cursory research will show you that certain foods leave people more satisfied for much longer than other foods. So rather than "just eat bell peppers" or something else tortuous, you may learn through research and for yourself what foods are likely to make you less hungry, and try eating those. For myself, I've learned that two boiled eggs in the morning leaves me only peckish by the time lunch comes around. It is one way I impact the problem of feeling hungry without compromising my other goals.

To be a great problem-solver, you'll make a habit of gleefully digging into the fundamentals.

## NOW: DIG INTO THE FUNDAMENTALS

Time to practice digging into the fundamentals! If you have a current problem, go figure out how the system works: make direct observations, flick through the manual, do research online. Just make sure you're understanding the highest-level variables, rather than learning everything about it.

If you're not currently working on a problem, go remind yourself how your toilet works. Lift the lid off, have a look. Learn about it, then go explain it to somebody. And if that's not challenging enough, try to figure out your car gearbox.

**CHAPTER 6**

# Don't Rely on Experts

*Doveryai, no proveryai (trust, but verify).*

—OLD RUSSIAN PROVERB,
MADE FAMOUS BY PRESIDENT RONALD REAGAN

Experts are wonderful people to have around. I know that's probably not what you're expecting to read at the beginning of this chapter. But it's true, and I mean it sincerely. Just don't rely on them.

When solving hard problems, you're going to come up against something you don't know or understand. I have read some manuals in my time and found spots where I wasn't able to make heads or tails of what I was looking at. Sometimes the science is hard enough that it's just too far out of your training or smarts to absorb quickly. These are moments where it's critical to utilize experts to help you solve hard problems. Asking the right person a few great questions can also save you hours reading boring technical manuals or dry science books. You'll want to work with people familiar with whatever you're trying to fix (a physical asset, a management procedure, a piece of software, etc.), and you may need someone who has spent years researching a particular science that you haven't, from chemical engineering to psychology.

Specifically, these expert folks are called subject-matter experts, or SMEs. They are highly experienced in a certain field, and have earned their status by understanding something very deeply and demonstrating that consistently. These experts are operators and

77

mechanics of a certain asset, such as accountants, IT experts, lawyers, equipment suppliers, political polling consultants, personal trainers, psychologists, and therapists. These experts are likely to know much more than you do about a specific topic and have a lot to teach you. They deserve your respect and attention.

My dad is one of these people. He worked for over 30 years as a university professor teaching metallurgy. During my childhood, we'd walk through Hong Kong and he'd point at rusty things and tell me how they were corroding. Now it's hard for me to walk around a city and not see all of the corrosion happening. I learned a lot from him and deeply appreciate the wealth of knowledge he has, and the value he brings.

My dad has frequently been asked to help in situations in which something broke catastrophically, and the insurance company was trying to figure out what went wrong. This might be figuring out why an elevator cable snapped or why a crane fell off a building. He'd study the situation, perhaps inspect components under a high-powered microscope, clarify the way in which it broke, what stresses were put on it, and why it didn't handle those stresses.

My dad is not just an SME; he is also a great problem-solver. It's very handy when both come in one package, but that is not always the case. Your SME may or may not be a great problem-solver, and you need to be very careful with confusing the two.

For easier problems, experts can make some faster experience-based guesses than you probably can. They'll be able to spot some patterns you may have missed, or may have just seen an almost-identical problem before, and if they're right in their educated guess, they can save you a lot of time.

When solving hard problems, experts may or may not help you progress. You can end up in a blind alley, or they can simply say it's impossible, and kill progress altogether. It all depends on how you work with them to get the best out of them and avoid some of the potential pitfalls. You should utilize experts, but not rely on them.

The difference is a subtle one, but very important. Utilizing an expert means asking them questions that will help you understand a science, process, or asset; it means getting their help in clarifying information you're seeing, or knowing where to find information you need. Relying on an expert means handing them the reins; it means giving them responsibility for solving the problem or declaring it impossible; it means giving them authority so their guess or conclusion is what you or your organization blindly follow.

## WHY PEOPLE RELY ON EXPERTS

People often rely on experts when they're not confident that they can make rapid progress to solve a hard problem. Typically, they believe it will be a quicker, easier, safer path. They've had experiences where SMEs have solved some easier problems, and are assuming they're facing the same set of circumstances with harder ones. And indeed, if your only problem-solving tool available is guessing, a good expert might be the best guesser you have available, as they can guess with experience.

But with hard problems, the circumstances are very different. When getting help, you need to understand if you're hiring a great problem-solver who happens to know that subject, or if you're hiring a subject-matter expert who may well help you.

People also hope that the expert will give them political cover. This cover can protect a team or leader from outside regulators, internal scrutiny, or your boss. Bringing in an expert demonstrates that you're taking action, and if they declare that a problem needs money thrown at it to be resolved, the heat is off your back. Even in situations where political cover is required, good problem-solvers will focus on getting to the root cause of the problem and implementing the actual solution. They will happily utilize the SMEs in this pursuit.

## THE PITFALLS OF RELYING ON EXPERTS

Once an expert decides something, it can be very difficult to challenge the decision. If they're right, and you're not a very good problem-solver anyway, that's fine. You have certainty and comfort, and it happens to be the right solution. The problem is when they get things wrong or set off on an unproductive path, which is much more likely when working on hard problems. An expert is often positioned so that their opinion is worth more than yours. To challenge that, even with the right facts, can be quite frightening for them. When you ask an SME to *solve the problem for you* rather than help you understand specifics, you become wholly reliant on them.

You might get lucky: Your SME might happen to be a good problem-solver. But more often than not, they just guess like everyone else, because they've solved a lot of easy problems this way in the past. Asking them to just solve your hard problem for you is unlikely to lead to an elegant solution.

There are three particular factors that can put SMEs in a particularly bad position to be great problem-solvers for you or your organization. The expert may:

- Feel they need to have a rapid answer.

- Be misaligned.

- Have the "curse of knowledge."

## RAPID ANSWERS

The first danger to relying on an expert is their reputational need to have a rapid answer. "Hey, we brought you in: You're the expert in the field, what's the answer!?" This puts pressure on an expert to guess at a solution right away.

An SME is valuable because they know things, and know them very thoroughly. Demonstrating that value means demonstrating that they know something very deeply, and whether this is helpful or not, it often means avoiding showing that they *don't* know something. The implicit belief for many SMEs is that admitting their ignorance of a detail will damage others' confidence in them. When you ask them for an answer, they are much more likely to give you *an* answer than say, "I don't know."

In the case of my friend's mom's car, the dealer experts had guessed that "there might be a software bug" or "maybe there was a short-circuit," and so passed the buck to the shop, which found nothing. Others told her that *nothing was wrong,* because they couldn't just say, "I don't know." It wasted an incredible amount of time, and she considered using the lemon law to swap out her car.

## MISALIGNMENT

Second, there is often a basic conflict of interest between an SME and you or your team, regardless of whether the SME is internal or external to your organization. A good example is a vendor. How they get paid may color their view of the solution they think you need. This doesn't have to be a matter of dishonesty or moustache-twisting villainy, but simply a subconscious bias.

If you bring in a supplier of hardware or software to look at a problem you're having with an older model, you have to keep in mind that not only is it their job to sell you a newer model, but they've probably already sold themselves on why that newer model is going to be the best thing for you. If you have a new product and can't make enough of it, a supplier that you call in for help may quite naturally and honestly suggest you buy a new or parallel bottleneck asset, and show you that the ROI (return on investment) for the purchase is positive.

A more interesting kind of misalignment is the risk-reward calculus for the expert and your organization. Often, SMEs are fundamentally conservative: Their reputation depends on not screwing something up. A hundred happy customers lead to referrals, but a single very irate one can kill a career. It is critical to avoid the risk of being blamed if anything goes wrong.

Isn't some risk-aversion a good thing? Yes, if the risk and reward are all in the same place. But most SMEs are positioned to be conservative by spending *your* money.

A few years back, I was investing in a couple of single-family homes for rent. It's quite common in this situation to set up a limited liability company (LLC) to protect your other assets in case something goes wrong with these investments. Someone might trip and fall down the stairs in one of your rental homes and then sue you, wiping out everything you own. Often, people set up separate LLCs for each property they own, so if there's a problem in one, it doesn't impact any of the other rental homes.

When I was structuring my investment, I instructed my lawyer to set up one LLC for both rental properties. The reason is that I hate paperwork, and two LLCs sounds like twice as much paperwork as one! I also did my research on the likelihood of being sued, and it turned out to be very small. As it happens, I did this research by talking to a friend who is an industry expert. The calculations we did showed I was over 1,000 times better off on average just having both in one LLC.

The lawyer was of course very insistent that I create two LLCs, and it took a lot of fortitude to prevent that from happening. Luckily, I've had some experience at effectively managing experts. The lawyer would have been paid twice as much for two LLCs, but I don't think this was the motivation. It's a more conservative move, but no business person should make the decision to have two LLC's in this situation. You can imagine that if the lawyer sets up 10,000 of these and one goes wrong, that's the story that gets reported: He might have gotten "burned" had he recommended a single LLC for multiple houses, and his client lost both houses in a lawsuit rather than one. It's easy to be conservative with other people's money: Don't ask SMEs to make business decisions for you without stepping back and considering a possible conflict of interest.

## CURSE OF KNOWLEDGE

One danger of relying on subject matter experts is that their extensive experience can be a mental hindrance to solving a unique, hard problem. The "curse of knowledge" is a cognitive bias that leads people highly informed about a topic to be unable to think about it in a fresh way, with a fresh pair of eyes.

SMEs are good at quickly finding patterns in familiar territory. This can be very powerful for solving easier problems, but for harder problems this can be their downfall. As with other prejudices, they can miss or ignore data that doesn't fit their previous conceptions. This tendency can cause them to jump to conclusions, and those can be very hard to challenge. Going back to my lawyer setting up the LLC, this could be a simpler explanation of what happened. He was so accustomed to providing separate LLCs for houses that it may have been hard for him to even consider an alternative.

## HOW GREAT PROBLEM-SOLVERS UTILIZE EXPERTS

When you encounter the harder problems that typically occur in more complex processes and systems, subject-matter experts can speed you on your way. They can give you answers to questions, help you build out what variables control the problem, and point you to the parts of the system that will yield insight.

So how do you utilize experts properly? The first rule is *stop asking them to solve your problem.* Don't ask them, "what's causing this?" Ask them questions such as, "help me understand how this piece works" (see Table 6.1) Get them to point you in the right direction for the resources you need to understand the system. When you are dealing with them, focus on the specific variable that you're working on: how to measure it, and what variables control it. A well-positioned SME will be invaluable in helping you more quickly find the answers to the right questions. And when you have them on board, they'll help you come up with a very elegant solution if it requires their technical skill.

| Table 6.1: Don't rely on subject matter experts to solve your problems. | |
|---|---|
| DON'T... | DO... |
| Simply ask them what the answer is. | Get their help understanding how things work. |
| Ask them what their best guess is. | Learn what they notice when they are smelling the problem. |
| Ask them what you should do next. | Ask them where in the process to look to find the information you need. |
| Expect them to solve your problem for you. | Thank them for their help! |
| Let them block you from a needed path of inquiry. | Recruit their help in removing roadblocks. |
| Let them use their authority to direct you without the facts. | Ask them to help you get the data to back up any claims they make. |
| Let jargon be used that you do not understand. | Utilize them to explain specific knowledge. |

Remember that SMEs are humans, too, and might not be as good a problem-solver as you are. You need to use your skills and capability you've developed as a strong problem-solver to guide them. If they start guessing and brainstorming, bring them back to a more rigorous approach. If they state something as a fact and you don't see the evidence for it, help them dig deeper.

Get their help in handling technical terminology and jargon, which are often littered through the lexicon around any complex system. They can help you to understand how a system is supposed to work, what a data stream means, or what is scientifically going on. Asking them to help you understand a technical detail or phenomenon positions them and you to succeed.

There are times when people are so devoted to not relying on experts, that the pendulum swings too far the other way. This can lead to a "do it on your own, regardless of the outcome" attitude. I must confess this is a mistake I've personally made many times, in business and at home.

I remember a particularly embarrassing example when I decided to redo the drywall on part of a wall in my house, on my own. I figured, "I can do this! How hard can it be? It'll be quicker than contacting a skilled person to do it." Cutting the drywall and taping it wasn't too hard, but when it came to spreading the joint compound, I discovered I lacked the skill and patience for the job. So despite burning lots of time in rework, I ended up with a fairly bumpy, ugly wall. I should have gotten some help and training from someone who knew what they were doing.

We can imagine our relationship with an SME as something that exists along a spectrum, between radical self-reliance—in which we shut experts out—and total expert reliance—in which we give them responsibility to solve the problem. Finding the right position along this spectrum will accelerate the problem-solving process and achieve the simplest, most economical solution.

As you work with SMEs going forward, remember that they may not be better problem-solvers than you are. Regardless of this, if you want to become a better problem-solver, you need to learn how to work effectively with them, and not rely on them.

## NOW: DON'T RELY ON EXPERTS

Before you engage your next expert, decide what questions you want to ask them. Each of these questions should:

1. Be related to smelling the problem or digging into the fundamentals.

2. Not be asking for an opinion or solution, but instead for simple facts.

Set expectations with the expert up-front that you *aren't* asking them to solve the problem, but that you'll be frequently asking for clarifications of unclear terms that they use.

**CHAPTER 7**

# Believe in a Simple Solution

*Whether you believe you can do a thing or not, you are right.*

—HENRY FORD, AMERICAN INDUSTRIALIST

"Nat, you don't understand: This thing's got a mind of its own." I've been doing this work long enough that I have heard something like this more times than I can shake a stick at, about all kinds of problems. When people give human-like characteristics to inanimate objects, machines, and systems, they're typically choosing to believe that there is not a simple solution to the problem—or even one at all.

I've heard such declarations about people, too: "They're just not reasonable," or "I'm just not good at this"; and health issues: "My body is just finicky." By making it a mystery, you imply that you can't apply a rational approach to it. Any possible solution must therefore be very complex, so let's not worry too much about solving the problem and instead learn to live with it. It seems fairly clear to me that embracing this belief is going to lead to failure.

People mythologize hard problems in this way because it is comforting. If a problem becomes a supernatural titan, we can tell ourselves that there's something special about it that has kept us from solving it, rather than our lack of skill. If it's "more art than science," then we're no longer responsible for really fixing it at the root cause.

Great problem-solvers instead believe in a simple solution to hard problems, and that they can reach it with rigorous problem-solving. This belief puts responsibility for action front and center with nowhere to hide.

What do I mean by a simple solution? Once you understand the true root cause—the one or two variables that aren't operating appropriately in a complex system—you know specifically what's wrong. Here's how you can judge this: First, you and others can understand it because you have the cause-and-effect story laid out, without having to take the word of an expert. Second, you can deliberately make the failure occur.

## WHAT HAPPENS WHEN YOU BELIEVE IN A COMPLEX SOLUTION

I remember the daunting task of trying to organize my closet. My wife and I share a closet and we were starting to "overlap." I was having trouble keeping my different clothes sorted and fitting them all in. At the time, I *didn't* believe in a simple solution. I thought I had to go through big changes: change my organizing system or maybe store some stuff seasonally in the attic. As I considered my complex solution I found myself irritated with the situation. It was also easy to cast my eye over my wife's clothes and consider that perhaps the solution lay there.

A friend of mine who read a book on simplifying one's life said, "No, it's quite easy! Just get rid of the stuff you don't use! You won't have a storage or organizational problem." Once I realized this was possible, I cleared out what I didn't wear in 90 minutes. I picked up one T-shirt and realized it was probably my thirtieth-favorite or so. I decided to donate over half of my wardrobe that I rarely or never wore. Once I'd dropped it all off, I had empty drawers and shelves. It's now easy for me to find and pick what I'm going to wear, I only wear stuff I like, and all those extra items are now helping other people.

When you don't believe in a simple solution to a hard problem, you instead believe in a complex solution. These complex solutions are easy to come by, but they tend to be expensive. Instead of understanding what's causing something to break, you can often just buy a new one. Maybe that'll fix the problem, but maybe—in the case of the chemical facility's pump seals—it won't. So then you go for another complex solution, such as making the seals bigger. Or replacing them faster when they break. These complex solutions, when they work, are symptom-fixing instead of curing the disease. What's even more insidious is that your organization believes great work is being done, and that resources are being effectively deployed on high-priority items.

A classic example of a complex solution is on a factory floor where a piece of equipment is failing, and the organization reaches a consensus that it's time to buy a new one. You might think that this just requires money. And it certainly requires that: For any given factory, critical assets tend to be expensive relative to their revenue and cash on hand. Just buying something new often means taking on debt. But if you've never been to a factory floor, you can't imagine the complexity of the solution. Often these floors are packed tight with equipment, conveyors, pipes, storage racks, and electrical conduits. If you look at one of these floors and imagine what it's going to take to just get that machine out and put a new one in, it suddenly becomes daunting. This is the mess you face with a complex solution. Imagine if you were able to instead solve one or two problems on that asset so that it could meet the needs of the business for the next 10 years.

One chemical processing facility we were working with had a treatment plant that was designed to break down a dangerous chemical by-product into two inert ones. After some years, the facility was scrubbing less than 50% of the chemical: The rest of it still needed to be dealt with in some way. To "solve" this, they paid another company heaps of money to carry the by-product off to their own facility, where *they* would scrub it.

When some great problem-solvers attacked the problem, they believed the problem was due to a straightforward root cause. This resulted in them relentlessly smelling the problem and digging into the fundamentals until they measured airflow through a critical point in the scrubber, and found it was way too low.

This led them to take out the flow pipe and observe it: They found that the pipe had been clogged by corrosion due to humidity, so there was very little air blasting through (which was process-critical). They were able to clean the pipe and put a dehumidifier on the intake, and their facility was back up and running. Once found, implementation was much easier on the organization and its P&L (profit and loss) than the work-around of processing the material elsewhere.

## WHY PEOPLE BELIEVE IN COMPLEX SOLUTIONS

To understand the drivers of this more deeply, let's look at most people's direct experiences with attempts to solve hard problems. Consider that most people are accustomed to poor problem-solving, which will always yield a more complex and difficult solution than good problem-solving. In many organizations, people are so used to this pattern that they have come to believe that complex problems *must* have a complex solution. The first time many people are exposed to a simple, elegant solution, they can react badly: they'll assume that a simple solution meant that the problem was simple, and somebody must have been an idiot to allow it to occur or persist. Therefore many organizations have formed political pressure to *suppress* belief in a simple solution to a hard problem.

If you want to be a great problem-solver, you need to resolve this issue in your mind now. If you believe that complex solutions are better than simple ones, or if you believe it's better to take a simple guessing shortcut, but then be saddled with a horrendous, complicated execution plan, you might as well give up now. For those of you on the fence, consider the possibility that there may be many more simple solutions out there, hidden by tough problem-solving, than you've ever believed to exist.

## WHAT HAPPENS WHEN YOU BELIEVE IN A SIMPLE SOLUTION

Say you sometimes don't sleep well; perhaps you're taking sleeping aids to help. There's a risk of forming an addiction to these and of course you do not really know what is going on. Contrast this with: "Whenever I eat cheese at dinner, I don't sleep well," because it turns out you're mildly lactose intolerant. You can test this, because on the days you eat cheese, you don't sleep well; when you cut out cheese, you sleep fine.

Your simple solution, resulting from solving the hard problem correctly, will always give you the most effective outcome, whatever your goal.

If you believe in this simple solution, your behavior is going to change. First, you're going to attack the problem rather than work around it, because you can envision a future in which the problem is fully, economically, simply solved. Second, you're not going to settle for complex solutions. If you believe your shrink-wrapper might be tearing your bags because there is something as simple as a loose bolt that interferes with its function, you're not going to put up with the expense of buying a new one and replacing the machine.

Don't confuse believing in a simple solution with hoping that a simple guess will work. That mostly leads to failure. Look at weight loss: Various friends have tried all of these to no avail:

- Perhaps I am overweight because I did not own a treadmill.

- Perhaps it is because I eat fat in my diet.

- Perhaps it is because I do not have a personal trainer.

- Perhaps it is because I need to skip a meal.

- Perhaps I need to starve myself and then have "cheat days."

You can no doubt add to this list. This isn't how you solve a hard problem like body weight. My friends, along with many others, had tried and failed to solve their problem because they guessed at many solutions: some were complex; others were just way off the mark.

All of these folks lost weight because they came to believe there was a simple solution and got to problem-solving; this enabled them to actually do the work to figure out the root cause of their problem. They didn't use any of those "one weird trick" nonsense fads; they built a solution based on an understanding of the fundamentals behind their struggles.

In my own home, I used to struggle with the toilet paper always running out. I had tried asking people to be more vigilant, but it was a complex solution that didn't work and caused unnecessary strife. Instead, I just bought a tower (see figure 7.1): this way, the toilet paper rarely ran out, and we knew well ahead of time when we were reaching emergency reserves.

Fix the problem with a much simpler solution.

**Figure 7.1: A much simpler solution**

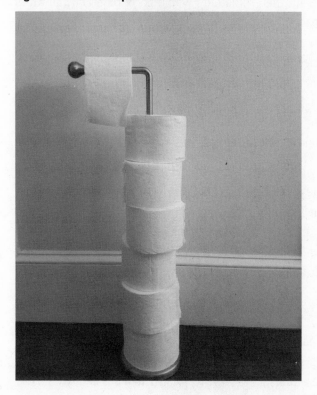

I was helping a company once that made plastic tubes for high-end cosmetics. The tubes were made on one machine, and then transferred onto pins that were connected to long, rotating chains, so they could air-cool. The next step in the process was to print the appropriate design onto the tube. For this to happen, the tube had to be loaded onto the printer. This involved the tube being blown off the pin onto a vacuum manifold that sucked it into position and then loaded it into the printer.

The problem was that the tubes would sometimes miss the manifold and fly off because the pins weren't always straight, or the chain would get slightly out of sync. I remember this poor mechanic who had to spend a lot of time every week straightening the pins so the tubes would fire true; the pins were bent because every now and then something would go wrong, and the tubes would fly past the spot they were supposed to fall into. There was a lot of discussion about how to make sure all of the pins were always perfectly straight—something that seemed impossible to achieve. There was talk about changing out the entire system, but there was mostly a sense of hopelessness and resignation that their current solution of the mechanic spending a lot of his time on this mundane and unrewarding task was now a way of doing business.

By studying the problem properly, and understanding the critical variables, I was able to come up with a permanent solution that took half an hour to implement. We put in a large backstop so that even if the tube missed the manifold by a significant margin, it would bounce back and fall into place. It was a pretty simple and elegant solution. It made the mechanics a lot happier.

I can anticipate some skepticism here: "What if there *isn't* a simple solution?" I want you to consider what that might mean. Can we understand the levers of physics, chemistry, or biology that dictate something's behavior? Absolutely. Could there be a case where understanding the root cause to a problem would not lead to a simpler solution than if we didn't understand the root cause? There might be, but it won't yield a *more* complex one.

If you *don't* believe in a simple solution, you are very unlikely to find it, whether it is there or not. And usually, it's there. So if you want to become a great problem-solver, you need to develop the belief, and therefore adopt the behaviors, that there is a simple solution. The only way to do this is to go find evidence for yourself.

When I'm training problem-solvers, this is an iterative process where we build momentum. As people find elegant solutions to problems that seem more daunting, they're able to grow their confidence and tackle ever-harder ones. You've got to start solving some easier problems to root cause, and then graduate to harder ones. Where you struggle with this at the start, find an appropriate mentor to guide you in having those experiences.

## CELEBRATING SIMPLE SOLUTIONS

Simple solutions can be misunderstood in many situations—people will think that a simple solution meant a simple problem, and that its presence meant someone really screwed up. Imagine just walking into the boardroom of the toilet paper company saying, "All of our supply problems were due to a loose bolt!" Or walking into the director's office of the chemical processing facility saying, "Our expensive environmental discharge problem was due to a rusty pipe!" It might not fly over so well.

Truly great problem-solvers powerfully communicate the value of the problem-solving process and difficulty of the problem once the solution is found. To those unfamiliar with solving hard problems, a simple solution can look like a bad thing, so make sure you explain the problem-solving process that took you to your solution.

In business situations I train people to report their findings in the following way: First, start with data that shows the problem is solved—the clear result. After all, who cares otherwise, and it's cruel to keep people wondering while you share. Then start from the beginning and run through the problem-solving method that you have used. As a reveal, share the simple solution at the end.

Life's just better when you believe you can resolve something, and it's even better when you believe you can resolve it in an elegant and simple way. When you are certain of the root cause and have a simple, elegant solution to bring to bear, implementation will be much easier: Your solution will be economical and attractive, and you'll be able to give your organization or family confidence that the solution will yield a much better outcome.

## NOW: BELIEVE IN A SIMPLE SOLUTION

Remind yourself of a situation where you solved a problem and it was a lot simpler than you had thought it would be. Perhaps you had an issue with someone and thought they were going to "explode" when you raised it with them. It actually turned out okay. Keep that story in mind as you search for other simple solutions to the problems you're tackling.

CHAPTER 8

# Make Fact-Based Decisions

*There are in fact two things, science and opinion;*
*the former begets knowledge, the latter ignorance.*
—HIPPOCRATES, ANCIENT GREEK FOUNDER
OF THE SCIENCE OF MEDICINE

The 2002 Oakland Athletics baseball team had a hard problem that you may be familiar with. They were losing game after game, their best players were about to leave as free agents, and their budget was too tight to sign on new big-ticket players to carry the team. If the Athletics were going to be good, they needed talent on a budget.

Traditionally, baseball scouts would assess the value of talent based primarily on intuition and experience. They had seen a lot of baseball—many had played—so they believed they had a pretty good sense of what a good player looked like. They only used high-level metrics like runs batted in (RBI) and batting average, combining these with subjective assessments of a player's swing and stance. Ultimately, the recruiting decisions they made were all opinion-based, and didn't factually connect to teams winning games. This created a particular complication to recruiting. Due to a lack of facts, a "herd mentality" could take over: When a few scouts started showing interest in a player, that player became more valuable to the eyes of other scouts, and thus their price would go up. The Athletics' scouts couldn't compete in this situation.

A young Harvard economics grad named Paul DePodesta proposed the radical notion that scouting and recruiting decisions could be made with hard facts, connecting player statistics directly with team wins. Specifically, he proposed using a "sabermetric" approach based on the player's on-base percentage to assess talent. This new approach helped the Athletics to scoop up consistent, but under-rated, talent at a very cheap price and build out a strong team on a tight budget. The next year, they went on to win 20 games in a row, setting a Major League Baseball record. The Boston Red Sox copied this approach to win the 2004 World Series, and it's now standard practice across the League.

This story was told in *Moneyball,* which is both a book and a movie.[1] What I find so interesting about it is just how much resistance DePodesta faced. The Athletics' scouts were so accustomed to making decisions with opinions that they simply couldn't imagine fact-based decision-making in their scouting process. They ridiculed and opposed DePodesta at every step. Talking heads across the league criticized his approach. Almost everyone fervently insisted that intuition and experience were the only ways by which to make these recruiting decisions. Brand was vindicated in the end, but it's a great lesson in how hard it can be to champion facts in problem-solving.

When solving your own hard problems, you're going to have decision points where, invariably, opinions are going to pop up. If you're working with a team, each member may have different opinions. Great problem-solvers also have opinions; what makes them different is that they recognize them for what they are and then set them aside.

What do I mean by "fact-based decisions" versus "opinions?" Let's say you're ordering pizza for the office. You might say, "I think most people are going to want pepperoni or cheese." That's your opinion. If you poll the office, you might find something else:

that would be fact-based. Even a statement such as, "Last time we ordered, all the pepperoni and cheese were gone, and we had 2 extra Hawaiians," would be a fact-based observation from which you could make a better decision. Yes, it's that simple.

I'm not expecting the thought "Hey, make fact-based decisions!" to be an earth-shattering conceptual revelation. It seems like the sort of thing that should go without saying. But it's not something most people are good at. It's probably a little bit like your doctor telling you that your road to good health involves eating better, sleeping more, and exercising. Sure, you know this.

The same goes for how you make decisions in problem-solving efforts. In my time, I've found that across business, personal life, and government, many people don't use facts at all, especially when there are particular motivators to avoid them. But most people believe they're making fact-based decisions, when they are, in fact, making opinion-based ones.

## OPINION-BASED DECISIONS IN DISGUISE

Most opinion-based decisions are made under the disguise of being fact-based decisions. Pre-2004 baseball scouts certainly believed they were making fact-based decisions: They went out and watched the players hit and field balls; they saw fitness combine reports. The problem is they had some observations in front of them, and then applied their opinions to make decisions.

A common way this masquerade is done in business is to use the "wisdom of the group" or the wisdom of experts (internal or external) to make decisions. One might have a vote, or a subjective way of ranking different ideas based on our opinions of what might be going on. This kind of decision-making is actually encouraged by some problem-solving approaches.

Imagine we're deciding what restaurant to go to. We might gather a "consensus opinion" about where people want to go; the idea being that the greatest average happiness will come from the most popular pick. The wisdom of the group works well for maximizing preferences, but unfortunately it is carried forward to other situations that are wholly inappropriate. If you were in a hospital you would not grab 10 random people and have a vote on where to make an incision for a surgery. A good surgeon will use the facts of their patient and their knowledge of anatomy to choose where to cut.

The odd thing about this restaurant example is that the facts *are* people's preferences about what restaurant they want to go to. The problem definition is: "We don't know which restaurant most people will be happy at." Getting a consensus of opinion is actually gathering the facts on that problem. There are cases in which the goal is to maximize preferences: in these, preferences are valid facts. When that's not the goal, focusing on people's opinions won't solve the problem.

Sometimes problem-solvers will use their assumptions about facts, or the assumptions of others, to make decisions, rather than verify the facts themselves. This is a particular problem when something is "known to all." Of course one of the great problem-solving battles of our time is the battle of the waistline. If you're my age, you may remember, "No fat touches my lips, no fat touches my hips." Turns out this is total nonsense. You can get facts about how much weight something will put on you by reading the calories on the packaging of different products.

Sometimes people intentionally hide or pervert facts. They do this for political reasons: They find the conclusions drawn from the facts inconvenient for their personal agenda. This obviously happens in national and local policy discourse—and I'll let you think of your own examples here, as I'm sure you're aware of many—but it happens in businesses and families, too.

## PITFALLS OF OPINION-BASED DECISION-MAKING

In business, you see people getting into all kinds of trouble around this. They get a group to brainstorm a big list of ideas of what people want to work on. Then they run a prioritizing session about what to do first, often based on people's subjective opinions. Perhaps everyone gets to vote for three things on the list and the items with the most votes win. Wouldn't it be better if they mathematically worked out which of the ideas could have the greatest objective impact and prioritize based on that? We can do this by using facts to determine which is most objectively valuable for the business.

Opinion-based decision-making stymies progress when it's misapplied to practical problems. For instance, people in my town are much more worried about whether there's a gun in your home when they drop their kid off for a play date, than whether you have a swimming pool. Guns are scary! Pools are fun! One is more likely to kill your kid than the other: Do you have an emotional reaction about which it is? Same goes for sharks: They're also scary! Every now and then, a shark appears on Cape Cod. People go crazy. They're far more worried about this than the drunk drivers heading back from dinner. If you want to keep your kids safe, and you don't prioritize your efforts to do so based on the facts, you're going to waste resources and perhaps needlessly endanger those you love. People believe it's perfectly factual to worry about sharks; they've seen shark bites and know for a fact that sharks can kill people. But that doesn't mean they're making decisions based on the appropriate available facts.

Life gets painful both at work and at home when you're not making decisions with facts. When all you hear are people's opinions, you're in the unenviable position of having to decide whose opinion to accept and invest in based on who you trust. You may have to consider who has a bias and who has an agenda. Until you have your problem-solving sorted out with a focus on facts, you're going to be stuck in this difficult situation.

## CHALLENGING OPINIONS

Some folks have asked me how to challenge people on the facts of a case without upsetting them. I'll say first that in my experience, asking someone to clarify for you where they got their facts is less fraught than having to choose whether to trust one person or another. But my quick advice here is to ask how as a team you would justify a decision to an outside body: What facts would we need to make our case? That can position you as working together, rather than implying that you don't trust somebody.

Whether we're trying to solve a problem of technology, business, or health, great problem-solvers are satisfied by nothing but the ground facts (see Table 8.1). They're ferocious and persistent about getting them. They don't accept anyone's opinion or assumptions about the truth. They are able to build consensus throughout the problem-solving process by justifying decisions at each stage with relevant facts.

## GOOD AND BAD FACT-FINDING

Digging up information that yields insight and decision is the backbone of any problem-solving effort: You're there to learn the necessary facts to understand what to change or fix. The right efforts to find facts will yield tangible steps down the path towards the root cause; poor fact-finding will confuse you and lead you astray.

One time we were working with a specialty manufacturing business that sold components to other businesses. The default plan was to move its operations from Western Europe to Eastern Europe to take advantage of lower labor costs. The facts on that half of the ledger were clear, but they hadn't checked the other side, and almost made a big mistake.

When they got the facts about how the move would affect their order fulfillment times, they found that these would increase significantly. They also found, when polling their most valuable customers, that short fulfillment times were a priority for most of them, and that the current fulfillment times were a big driver in why these customers were so loyal. They canceled the move, and not only saved a lot of time, money, and up-front investment, but they pivoted that investment to reducing their fulfillment times further, which enabled them to adopt a premium market position and increase profit margin in an otherwise near commodity sector.

## DIGGING INTO THE DATA

First, you'll need to verify that the information you're gathering is actually representative of reality. Particularly in data-rich environments, great problem-solvers will challenge whether sensor streams, studies, and so on are providing facts. Often problem-solvers face "data" that has been highly processed and may no longer represent the relevant reality on the ground.

A few years back some of my team were working at a performance coatings company that had the phone ringing off the hook with angry customers. Some of these customers got so frustrated that they switched suppliers. The customer service folks knew anecdotally that some customers were complaining about late shipments, but the management data told them that their in-full-on-time (IFOT) rate was 98%. That means that 98 out of

100 times a customer asks for an order it is shipped at the right time with nothing missing from it. This was a top rate result in this industry so it led to some confusion. Perhaps having 1 in 50 orders short or late was no longer an acceptable service level?

When we checked the customer service call logs, we found almost all the problems were about late shipments, so we became suspicious of the report's accuracy. The team dug into the code with a few shipping reports, and found that the system calculated IFOT by the final adjusted scheduled delivery date, rather than the initial requested one. Customer service managers were negotiating dates they could make with customers and these "updated" delivery dates were used to build the report. When the team fixed the code, they found that IFOT was only 37%, and were able to use that correct calculation to find critical patterns about the problem across the network that helped solve the key problem— understandably, angry customers.

## GETTING THE CONFIDENCE LEVEL RIGHT

You'll also have to pick the right level of confidence you need when determining whether the information you're seeing is representative of fact. I've seen people shoot both too high and too low here. Some folks I've worked with felt like they needed very high statistical confidence before testing something that was very low-cost and low-risk. I've seen others take a single measurement and decide a variable was in spec (that is, within a range in which the problem wouldn't occur), when it in fact varied frequently over time.

This stuff happens at home of course. A few months ago I found that some half-moon cookies were disappearing from the kitchen at an alarming rate. I have four kids, and sometimes they'd have a few for a snack or dessert. Each value-sized container we bought should have lasted a week, but they were disappearing within 2 days.

One evening I was walking through the house when I heard a noise from the kitchen. With kids in the house you are used to noises all the time and don't pay attention to them. However, this noise had "kid hiding something" written all over it, so I crept in to bust the culprit. My youngest had her hand literally in the cookie jar. I could have assumed that she was responsible for all the missing cookies with her bedtime snack, and she would have been most upset at the injustice of that. However, it seemed unlikely that she was snaffling 10 extra cookies each night: The one correct observation that she was responsible for some of the loss did not mean we had all the relevant facts. Of course, her older brothers were behind most of the disappearances, as I confirmed later.

| Table 8.1: Opinions versus facts. | |
|---|---|
| *Opinion* | *Fact* |
| "There are too many people on the planet." | "There are over 7 billion people on the planet." |
| "This is the decision most people think will be profitable." | "This decision has the highest projected return on investment." |
| "This person's behavior is self-destructive." | "I feel concerned about the behavior I've seen." |
| "The subway is really slow." | "It takes 30 minutes to go across town on this line and I would be happier if it were less." |
| "This machine is too old." | "The machine is 32 years old and it is hard to obtain spare parts." |
| "You are running it too fast." | "Above 60 units per minute 1% of the product is defective." |
| "We tried that before and it won't work." | "We tried that before and observed the following problem." |

## CHECKING FOR RELEVANCE

The facts you seek should also be highly relevant to your problem. So often, I see people bury themselves in mounds of data coming off their computers, hoping that some stream or other will yield an interesting correlation. There's nothing wrong with using statistical analysis as a tool, and with this ability to crunch big data, the cost of this continues to drop. However, recognize that relying on this is just guessing.

So what is a relevant fact? It's a fact that's going to answer the question you're asking that takes you to the next step in your problem-solving process. When you've reached a certain variable, you need to get the facts to accurately understand its behavior, and what controls it. Don't get distracted running about trying to measure everything you see.

"Back in the day," before the advent of cheap sensors and big data, great problem-solvers were skilled at getting facts. To be a great problem-solver today, you shouldn't lean blindly on data streams. When you have to take the time to go measure something yourself, your brain may be more prone to considering precisely what you're measuring and why, rather than default to grabbing what's immediately available. In part, this is a matter of focus and discipline.

## AVOIDING CONFIRMATION BIAS

The last major risk to getting good facts is our own prejudices. While we may not always test a solution based on our opinions or assumptions about what's causing the problem, confirmation bias can plague any problem-solving effort. I'm sure you've seen it in both corporate and government politics before. Great problem-solvers know how to recognize when their emotions or prejudices are getting in the way.

One morning I was helping get the kids ready for school only to find that one of them was apparently sick. I was quite suspicious as he was not getting on so well at school, and he had to do something that day that didn't exactly excite him. I think it might have been recitation day. He had missed quite a bit of school and I felt he was suffering from senioritis. The staff at school all seemed aligned that he was just faking it.

My wise and patient wife decided to take his temperature, which until then hadn't been mentioned at this point during our "problem-solving" discussions. Lo and behold, he had a 101-degree fever. Not the end of the world, but the thermometer certainly confirmed a day at home. Getting the facts triumphed over opinion based on bias.

## MEASURING AT THE RIGHT PLACE AND RIGHT TIME

These behaviors tend to reinforce each other and that is true here. Digging into the fundamentals is going to ensure you understand the variables that you're meant to measure in the first place. Smelling the problem and establishing a strong pattern of failure will help you understand the context under which to measure a variable in order to yield insight. For example, if you're having heart problems in stressful situations, you'll want to measure how your heart works electrically when you are stressed outside of the doctors office. (For me being in the doctor's office would be sufficiently stressful!) If you need to measure air pressure on an intermittently failing blow-molder, make sure to measure it while your problem is occurring.

I introduce people to hard problems using case studies, and then head out to test new skills on real-life problems. This is a great way to train people to search for the right data and run the right tests. Fortunately, there is never a shortage of unsolved problems, but it does save an awful lot of time learning in a controlled environment rather than running amuck in the real world wasting resources.

There is no direct recipe for ensuring that what you're looking at is the right fact or not. Challenging the validity of your facts, avoiding assumptions and opinion, and measuring the right variable the right way, are all skills that need to be developed with practice.

## NOW: MAKE FACT-BASED DECISIONS

Pick a hard problem you face, or may actually be working on. Write down the relevant facts you know and also write a list of opinions that you see floating around—perhaps in your own mind. Now challenge your "facts" and see if some of them are really just your opinion or the result of confirmation bias. If you are brave enough, try this with a political issue and share it with some other people so they can help you review it.

CHAPTER 9

# Stay on Target

*Simplicity is the ultimate sophistication.*
—LEONARDO DA VINCI, 15TH-CENTURY PAINTER AND INVENTOR

In hard problems of complex systems, there may be thousands of potential variables to look at, and hundreds or thousands of potential root causes. Your journey towards the root cause is one fraught with distractions that can lead you on wild detours or to disaster. To solve a hard problem, you'll need to quickly and consistently focus your efforts. You'll need to take special care to stay on target, avoid distractions, and ensure that you're simplifying.

## THE PROBLEMS OF EXPANSIVENESS

What great problem-solvers do is find the root cause in a methodical way, using what they learn along this path to eliminate vast swaths of possible root causes and avenues of inquiry without actually having to study them directly. I can't emphasize enough how important and powerful this is. In most problem-solving efforts I see, the root cause analysis step is an *expanding* step, where many ideas are generated and then tested. This comes from the good intention of wanting to be exhaustive, thereby not missing anything: We might try to think of all possible root causes and test them.

In the moldy food example from Chapter 1, "Stop Guessing," the team had become paralyzed by expanding on the problem. By the time we arrived, they had created a list of over 200 potential root causes. They had worked through half of them with no solution in sight. In this effort, they had wasted months and hundreds of thousands of dollars, and created brand new problems on the line by testing out these solutions. When we applied a methodical approach of eliminating top-level subvariables, we were able to very quickly eliminate almost all of these guesses in a few days. By the way, the root cause was not even in their original list of 200 ideas.

This drive towards expansiveness is a natural instinct: We're socially trained to think of all possible risks, and all the ways that something might have gone wrong. If we don't have a better approach, this is the best one available. There are even a lot of formal problem-solving methods that actively encourage expanding possibilities when problem-solving. As I've said before, expansive thinking is wonderful when you're creating new things. But when you're solving a practical problem, it's completely unhelpful. Great problem-solvers instead reduce and eliminate possibilities in order to stay on target. They are masters of simplifying.

## STAYING ON TARGET

Recall from Chapter 5, "Dig Into the Fundamentals," the grass on our lawn was too long. We were able to determine that the height of the grass is determined by how tall it was the last time it was cut, its growth rate, and how much time has passed.

At this point it is tempting to go nuts expanding this tree, as it can feel satisfying or important to learn about something completely. But our job is to efficiently find the root cause. So instead of expanding each variable, we want to see if we can eliminate some of the "high level" variables right at the start. Each one we get rid of has many subvariables that sit below it and we can then ignore.

Because this is a made-up example, we can do some tricky stuff like pretend we have a growth-rate log for our grass. For argument's sake, let's say we've remeasured the rate of growth of our grass and it's the same rate every week, so it's not responsible for our new problem. We cut our grass last week, and we always cut it every week, but the grass has become too long anyway. So we can eliminate caring about grass growth rate or time completely, and avoid digging at all into the fundamentals that control these variables. This process is shown in Figure 9.1, with red X's representing out-of-spec variables, and green check marks representing on-spec variables.

At this point we've immediately eliminated almost all variables and potential root causes without having to explore them. We don't have to care about bugs, rain, sunlight, or any of that, and the problem has been simplified. Once we've eliminated both rate of growth and the time, then it has to be the case that the grass was too long when we last finished cutting it.

Since the grass was too tall when we last finished cutting, either our lawn mower blade was too high when we cut it, or the grass had deflected by too great an angle when the blade met the grass. Notice again that in the next step, we're keeping our scope simple, and limited to the highest-level controlling variables (see Figure 9.1).

**Figure 9.1: Variables controlling the length of grass at last cut (blank variables not yet measured)**

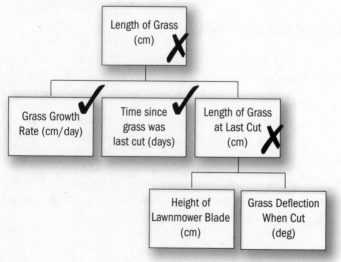

If we stay on target with these two variables, we'll find either that our lawn mower blade was too high, or that something was causing the grass to deflect (maybe a dull blade, wet grass, and so on).

That's the beauty of simplifying and staying on target: By eliminating the variables closest to the primary variable, we immediately eliminate many potential root causes, and we can avoid collecting data about or looking deeply into most of the process or system.

Of course for figuring out how to keep your lawn trimmed, this rigor isn't necessary. But as we move from very easy problems to very hard ones, the total number of variables involved in controlling our primary variable expands. Sometimes people resist this level of rigor: They are used to solving some easy problems quickly by jumping ahead, so they're tempted to do the same here, thinking it will be faster. It may be faster in "getting you doing something," but it doesn't get you to the true root cause sooner. I'd much rather you learn this here than learn it at the school for hard knocks when you hit the wall with a hard problem and everyone gives up on you.

## THE POWER OF SIMPLIFYING

Let's consider a more complex system that may have a root cause buried deep in the variable tree. By measuring and eliminating higher-level variables, you will see that we can ignore almost all variables at lower levels that control the problem. As shown in Figure 9.2 the X-marks represent off-spec variables we've measured; check marks represent on-spec variables we've measured; and white boxes represent the variables we never had to identify or measure at all, because they control on-spec variables—so we no longer care about them at all.

**Figure 9.2: The full variable tree with variables eliminated**

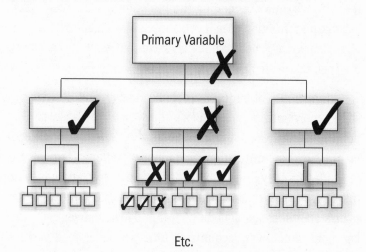

Etc.

Note how identifying on-spec variables high up in the tree cleaves off almost the entire set of possibilities right away: This is how you take impossibly complex systems and simplify them to become manageable and solvable. Many problem-solving methods don't support this behavior, and I highly recommend using one that does.

Let's consider instead a potential tree in which we've expansively determined all possible variables down to a very fundamental level, without eliminating anything at a higher level. We would have hundreds or thousands of variables to account for.

Imagine trying to measure and wrap your arms around all of those variables or guess at which ones are important: It's a bit of a ridiculous prospect. Luckily, you don't have to build these massive, sprawling trees in order to solve your problem. Staying on target means understanding and measuring only what you need to in order to drill to the root cause and find a simple solution.

Structuring your efforts in this way will give you the confidence to have tenacity. A great problem-solver will know that each step they take in understanding and simplifying the problem is getting them closer to understanding the root cause. They won't panic just because they don't see it yet, and they will maintain the discipline to not jump ahead when they have a guess. If they get stuck, they can take a step back.

This approach also means problem-solving teams can measure and demonstrate progress before they know the answer. They don't measure how many guesses they've tested; they measure progress by how much they have understood and eliminated or expanded, as they learn what variables are in spec and which are out of spec. This structure allows them to sanely organize their team's efforts, assign actions with due dates, and set goals they can hold themselves accountable to. Each understood variable, either eliminated or expanded, is a clear sign of major progress.

Let's look back at the toilet roll shrink-wrapper from the introduction. We knew what we had to look for because we had eliminated all other possibilities. We knew how the machine was designed to control the shape of the wrapping, and eliminated everything but a mysterious force at a certain point on the wrapper that caused the tear. Because we knew that this force *must* be responsible for the tearing plastic, the mechanic was able to look specifically for it, and then find it. I want you to appreciate that there was no way that guessing, would have come up with "maybe there's a random loose bolt that's vibrating its way into the wrapping cavity." Clear understanding of what was and was not happening enabled the specific focus required to resolve this issue.

When you move down your tree, keep in mind there may be multiple variables contributing to the failure. So if you don't eliminate all but one at a certain level, don't panic: You may have to go down multiple branches. Some problems require two off-spec variables to both be back in spec in order to be solved, where little or no progress is made adjusting only one. In one consumer-packaged plant I worked at, the arms that sealed bags closed (using heat and compression) were angled incorrectly in two separate dimensions, and changing only one didn't have a measurable impact on the problem. However, remember that when people start talking about a laundry list of things that have to be fixed, they are almost certainly guessing. You'll know it's not a laundry list when someone is able to demonstrate that these variables are out of spec, and explain physically how they directly contribute to the observed problem.

This iterative behavior of digging in, and then simplifying, is the on-target path to root cause. You'll know that you've found the root cause when you identify, understand, and measure the off-spec variable that is directly in your control to change (like "presence of bolt" or "cross-sectional area of seal flush pipe"). Knowing why it's out of control positions you to quickly develop an elegant solution. Don't "solve" your problem at a high level where you throw lots of money at it to make it go away: Stay on target and keep going until you've found the simple root cause.

## MISTAKES HAPPEN

A few years ago my microwave stopped working. It was completely blank, as if it had blown something internal. So I moved the plug to another power socket to check the power. That did not work. I put it back in the original socket and noticed the ground fault interrupt (GFI) had triggered. I reset it. The microwave did not work but I plugged in my phone to the second socket and there was power. Knowing that the power was now on and the microwave was still dead I concluded that something had fried inside and that event had probably triggered the GFI. So I paid a few hundred bucks for a new microwave, mumbling about how these things don't last the way they used to. When I plugged the new machine in it did not work either. I suddenly knew I had really messed this one up: What were the chances of two bad microwaves?

I studied engineering at college and no doubt a little extra "expertise" caused me to jump to a false conclusion. In my rush I had never actually checked the microwave in a live socket that I had checked with the phone. The root cause turned out to be a wiring fault in the first socket. I still have the spare microwave in my garage—turns out they last a long long time. Lessons in humility also last a long time.

You will make mistakes and incorrectly evaluate some variables. You need to be attuned to this and be prepared to go back, challenge, and fix your work.

## NOW: STAY ON TARGET

Things in life are always distracting you from the task at hand. Pay attention to this in the next day or so. Look for situations when someone is having a conversation about a topic, and people get distracted and end up talking about something completely different. Notice how you're taking care of one task and then find something else that needs fixing—such as loading the dishwasher and you notice the floor needs to be swept, and then moments later you're rearranging the closet. Noticing and eliminating distractions will enable you to stay on target when you're facing down your next complex problem.

## CHAPTER 10

# How to ChooseYour Method

*Choose wisely, for the true grail will bring you life; the false grail will take it from you.*[1]
—THE GRAIL KNIGHT, IN *INDIANA JONES AND THE LAST CRUSADE*

A few rare problem-solvers have a natural intuition for solving problems and have found success with limited outside structure or guidance. When we show them a good problem-solving approach they wonder what the big deal is and just get back to work.

For the rest of us mere mortals, the right kind of structure is critical, though without the right skills and behaviors it is insufficient. I've mentioned a number of times throughout this book that a strong problem-solving method will help you to consistently apply the behaviors we've covered. This is important for both when you face your next hard problem and when you're developing your skills on more moderate problems.

A strong method helps you in a few ways. First, it helps you apply the right behaviors while solving problems. Second, it gives you a consistent way to practice to improve more quickly. Third, it gives a common language and structure by which you can coach and be coached. Fourth, it helps you to redirect yourself when you get stuck, or backtrack when you have made a mistake. Finally, it helps you to tell your story in a logical way as you develop buy-in for your solution.

## CRITERIA FOR PICKING YOUR METHOD

I don't intend to tell you what should be the right problem-solving method for you. There are so many that it would be a bit silly for me to dig through all of them to give each one an individual assessment. Furthermore, different problem-solvers may just prefer some method over others because it fits their style. All of this is fine, as long as the method meets certain criteria that I discuss below. In the end as you hone your skills you will become less reliant on any one approach and will be able to adapt to the method that the other people around you are using. But as a great problem-solver, you'll need to insist on fiercely utilizing the behaviors you have worked so hard to ingrain.

Here is some guidance on what to look out for if you want to be able to solve hard problems.

First and foremost, **make sure the method you're choosing does not encourage guessing during its root cause analysis phase.** Almost all of them do, so this should eliminate most of your options right away. Unfortunately, most methods disguise the guessing stage in some fancy language, such as "determine possible root causes." This is making a list of guesses, and at this point I hope you would read such an instruction and declare, "How the heck am I meant to do that?" Even coming up with a "hypothesis" is a guess, despite it being a scientific term. If at any point in a method you are asked to make a list, "come up with" something, or hypothesize, then avoid such a method for the junk that it is.

Second, **look for a method that starts by focusing on the problem.** This will guide you to spend time getting close to the actual problem, understand what's really going on, and establish a pattern of failure. Some methods devote a few lines to this, and others many pages. Neither is strictly better than the other, and I've seen many methods that do this well. If you are primarily focused on developing your capability then you can quickly figure out how much guidance helps you. When choosing a method for a broader group, you need to strike a balance between keeping high-potential people engaged and not leaving beginning problem-solvers behind. If you want to solve hard problems, I suggest biasing towards the needs of the high-potential problem-solvers, and make sure you bring the others along as needed.

Watch out for methods that mostly focus on picking the right team members, getting buy-in, and so on. This is useful for political problems, especially ones that are zero-sum game in nature and where there is little agreement on the actual goal. However, this focus is not a core differentiator for solving hard process problems where there can often be fact-based alignment on the strategic goal. Similarly, endless focus on validating your solution typically implies a weakness with the method when actually identifying the true root cause.

In the end, **ask yourself whether the problem-solving method you're looking at is designed to encourage you to effectively use all of the problem-solving behaviors that you've learned.** Pick a good one, practice with it, use it to tell your problem-solving story, and you'll invariably develop and grow as a problem-solver. How do you know you have made the right choice? Measure progress in how you are developing your problem-solving skills, and most importantly, in the number of elegant solutions you successfully implement.

Keep in mind that the method you choose to guide you is of little use without strong problem-solving behaviors. Some methods will do more or less to guide you in applying some of the behaviors at the appropriate times, but most problem-solving behaviors should be applied throughout the entire journey (see Table 10.1). Just as the knife does not make the chef, neither will the method make you a great problem-solver. Practice by using one, but do not solely rely on it for your success.

## MANY METHODS ENCOURAGE GUESSING

In my own experience I have found that most problem-solving methods promote guessing at some point in the process, but that it is snuck in under disguise.

There are some typical broad steps to these problem-solving methods, whether or not they are good:

- Identify the problem and its pattern of failure

- Seek causes

- Implement the solution

Don't be lulled into a sense of security just because you have a structure that follows these high-level steps. At some point the vast majority devolve into guessing. Why is this? My best understanding is that there are two reasons: First, most people writing problem-solving books are so accustomed to guessing that it feels natural. But second, many problem-solving methods are designed to help people solve easy problems. You need motivated people willing to develop their skills in order to effectively use a problem-solving method that does not involve any guessing.

For easier problems, finding a pattern and then guessing is often enough to get by—you may be lucky and already have the data you need, or be able to easily guess where to measure and the pattern can yield the cause. **But whenever you read a method step such as "determine possible root causes," this is a red flag for your problem-solving method.** How are you meant to determine such a list? Pluck it out of thin air, or potentially worse, wait for someone else to do it?

| Table 10.1: The categories of problem-solving methods |
| :--- |
| *Which Kind of Problem-Solving Method Are You Using?* |
| **Structured guessing.** These very simple methods provide a bit of organizational structure to guessing, such as:<br><br>• Categorization (Fishbone Diagrams)<br><br>• Persistence (such as Five Whys)<br><br>• Collaboration (various forms of brainstorming)<br><br>They can accelerate progress in solving some easier problems. |
| **Pattern of failure.** These methods use more structure to help problem-solvers establish a strong problem description and pattern of failure. Typically, they include:<br><br>• A step-by-step series of questions to answer<br><br>• A step of determining with intuition some potential root causes to the problem<br><br>• Helping to improve the quality of guesses<br><br>• Preventing a problem-solver from guessing particularly unlikely potential root causes<br><br>These methods are helpful for moderate problems. |
| **First principles.** These methods may also contain structure that helps problem-solvers establish a strong problem description and pattern of failure. Their distinct features include:<br><br>• Pointing a problem-solver towards analyzing the controlling variables of the problem as black boxes (or independent elements)<br><br>• Iterating until a directly modifiable out-of-control element is identified as the root cause |

## VARIABLE ANALYSIS

Most problem-solving methods are not up to scratch and will not allow you to solve hard problems. The good news is there are several methods that will do the job. I will not list all of these, nor categorize others, as there are far too many to be comprehensive. Table 10.2 is a very brief description of Variable Analysis, which I use.

As you'll see, it's pretty light on instruction, and this is particularly true compared to some methods that are common in business today. One of the reasons I like it is that it is clearly a guide meant to encourage you to use the right behaviors, rather than something that implies that close adherence to very specific direction will get you there without thinking.[2]

| Table 10.2: Variable Analysis |
|---|
| 1. Define the problem.<br> a. What problem are you trying to solve?<br> b. Determine the primary variable<br> • Closely inspect the point of failure or failed output<br> • What measurable property do you want to change?<br> • Is it possible to define the problem using a more specific variable? |
| 2. Describe the problem: describe the problem in detail.<br> a. What does the problem look like?<br> b. When did the problem start?<br> c. How often does the problem occur?<br> d. Where does the problem first occur?<br> e. When where don't you see the problem? |
| 3. Create a variable tree: develop each layer of sub-variables by understanding how the process works<br> a. How is the process designed to control the primary variable?<br> b. What else determines the value of the primary variable?<br> c. Can we combine any of the sub-variables? |

4. **Eliminate sub-variables from the tree**
   a. What should the value of each sub-variable be to prevent the problem from occurring?
      - What is the relationship between each sub-variable and the primary variable?
   b. Eliminate sub-variables that do not contribute to the problem
      - What is the actual value of the sub-variable during failure? During non-failure?
      - What tests could you use to eliminate variables that are difficult to measure?
      - What does the pattern of failure tell you?
   c. Expand sub-variables that have not been eliminated (iterating step 3)
   d. Start with sub-variables that the pattern-of-failure suggests are most likely to contribute to the problem
   e. Continue to expand and eliminate sub-variables until you have found the out-of-spec variable(s) that are directly in your control
      - Can you explain exactly how the out-of-spec sub-variable(s) contribute(s) directly to the problem?
   f. If you get stuck...
      - Have you eliminated a sub-variable that you should not have?
      - Have you missed a sub-variable?

5. **Implement the solution**
   a. Implement the solution
   b. Verify the solution

I like this method for a number of reasons. First, variable analysis helps you remember to start by defining the problem well and getting to know the problem in detail, without consideration of what the potential solutions might be. Second, it guides you to only learn about the parts of the system that are out of spec and thus saves lots of time by ignoring the 90% to 95% of it that you never need to learn about in order to solve the problem. It does this by allowing you to rapidly discover which high-level variables are in control, so you can focus your attention elsewhere. Finally, it doesn't devote large attention to "ensuring the solution is sustainable," and so on, because if you have a clearly understood root cause, this is a relatively trivial step.

Even for great problem-solvers, structure is helpful as a pillar to lean on whenever you start to get off-course. It helps you refocus when you get stuck. Too much structure, though, becomes a rote checklist and disengages the brain, leaving no room for thinking or developing insight. Your structure should be your guide, rather than your recipe or puppet master.

## NOW: CHOOSE YOUR METHOD

If you have a method that you currently use, decide now whether it's robust enough to help you solve hard problems. If it is, wonderful! Keep going and practice those behaviors. If the method you use isn't strong enough, or you don't have a method at all, do a bit of research to find a method you like. Perhaps ask around with your friends to see what they find useful, and evaluate that.

Then go practice!

# CHAPTER 11

## Go Solve Some Problems

*It is possible, with lots of hard work, dedication, and timely help, to make a good writer out of a merely competent one.*[1]

—STEPHEN KING, *ON WRITING*

The whole point of this book is to help you develop your problem-solving ability and have you get out there solving more problems to root cause. Every person I have met is a problem-solver in their own lives and every single one also has untapped problem-solving potential. In this chapter, I want to discuss one last story that is currently one of my favorites.

My editor, Steve, was reading the manuscript for this book when he ran into a tricky problem in his house. He shared this story with me while giving me feedback on some of the early chapters.

Steve has a garage door opener to speed him in and out of his home. This is operated by a switch on the wall by the door into the house or by a remote controller that clips in his car. Recently the opener had developed a problem. It made a terrible racket when opening or closing the garage door and sounded like it was going to explode. He and his wife decided they needed to call a repairman to come help, which would have cost a couple hundred bucks.

However, when Steve read Chapter 2, "Smell the Problem," he decided, "Okay, I should go smell the problem." Normally, when he pressed the button he was in his car or by the door to the house, he wasn't close to the garage door itself, so he could only hear the racket. He decided to grab his remote out of the car and stand right by the door itself to see what was going on when it opened.

After a few openings, he found that the door was catching on something as it opened and closed, causing both shaking in the rails and struggling in the motor. When he looked closer, he found it was catching on a big garbage can, which had been moved too close to the door because a filing cabinet had somehow been pushed towards the garbage can.

Steve pushed everything back where it needed to be and communicated this "implementation" to his family to make sure it didn't get pushed back. Life was improved, money was saved, and Steve was thrilled.

You don't have to be a master problem-solver to get started solving the problems you come across in your life. When you face a problem, recognize that it is solvable and get stuck in it. Please send me your success stories!

## THE PROBLEM-SOLVER'S SCHIZOPHRENIA

My parting advice as you get started—and at all stages of your problem-solving adventures—is something that I've told the problem-solvers I've coached for years. It's certainly the case that if you don't believe you can solve a hard problem, you're going to give up as you run into trouble—and you *will* run into trouble. It's why they're called "hard."

But I've also found that blind confidence makes one lazy. If you believe that success is inevitable, you're less likely to work your tail off in order to achieve it. Hard problems are definitely immune to the power of belief. Simply deciding that you'll solve something doesn't solve it.

The best problem-solvers I know hold in their head a kind of contradiction. They simultaneously hold two beliefs: They have the skills needed to solve the problem, *and* they fear that this might be their moment of failure if they are not vigilant. They have the confidence to dive right in and get their hands dirty, to jump into unfamiliar situations, to explore processes or science that's brand new to them. And along with it, they know that there is no path to success laid out for them that they can follow. They must forge their own way, and they are wary of getting lost. They hate the thought of failure, and they know it's a real possibility.

This is "problem-solver's schizophrenia:" a fierce symbiosis of confidence and fear. Together, these will press you to stretch yourself, rather than stay back out of intimidation or laziness. They'll keep you moving forward into unknown territory, and keep you smart as you do this.

To develop the confidence, you'll simply need to practice, practice, practice, ideally with a coach that can provide help and feedback. To hold onto the fear, you just have to truly care about solving the problem. "Trying your best" shouldn't be your standard for personal success: Solving the problem should be.

## THE FINAL WORD

Practicing the behaviors in this book will help you build your problem-solving skills. On your journey to becoming a great problem-solver, you're going to have ups and downs. You'll make mistakes. But if you continue to develop your problem-solving behaviors, you will rack up a list of problem-solving victories that will drive you even further forward.

I can't guarantee you'll become the best problem-solver in the world. But however competent you are, and whatever your potential, I believe you can get even stronger. So put this book in your pocket, find someone to share the journey, and look for something important that needs fixing.

And get to it.

# NOTES

**INTRODUCTION**

1. Five Whys is a problem-solving method that encourages problem-solvers to explore beyond the most immediate apparent cause of a problem by asking what causes the apparent cause, what causes the secondary cause, etc, down to the 5th-level cause.

**CHAPTER 1**

1. Sir Arthur Conan Doyle, *Sign of the Four* (New York: Penguin Classics, October 2001), pg 16.

2. Lean and Six Sigma techniques are classic Business Improvement or Continuous Improvement techniques. A Fishbone Diagram is a cause and effect diagram that structures efforts to identify different types of potential causes of a problem.

3. The PackCorp scientific process was an early Process Improvement method, developed by PackCorp for internal use. It expanded upon early methods developed in Japan like the Toyota Production System (TPS) and was an early iteration of business problem-solving that influenced later methods like those used in Lean and Six Sigma..

4. Fault Tree Analysis is used to create a "tree" of factors that lead to a fault. It typically expands a fault or potential fault into two or more necessary conditions for a fault to not occur. Those conditions are in turn expanded by the conditions that are necessary to cause them to happen or not happen, etc, until the user has reached relatively fundamental conditions.

**CHAPTER 2**

1. Cheri Huber. *There Is Nothing Wrong With You.* (Chicago: Keep It Simple Books; October 1, 2001).

**CHAPTER 3**

1. George Lucas, *Star Wars: Episode V—The Empire Strikes Back* (20th Century Fox, 1980).

**CHAPTER 4**

1. W. Clemens Zinck, *Dynamic Work Simplification* (Malabar, FL: Krieger Publishing , 1971), pg 122.

2. Paul Polak, *Out of Poverty: What Works When Traditional Approaches Fail* (Oakland, CA: Berrett-Koehler, 2009).

3. Ibid., pg 9.

**CHAPTER 5**

1. Charles Duhigg, *The Power of Habit*. (New York: Random House Trade Paperbacks, January 7, 2014.)

2. In fluid dynamics, Bernoulli's principle states that an increase in the speed of a fluid occurs simultaneously with a decrease in pressure or a decrease in the fluid's potential energy. The principle is named after Daniel Bernoulli who published it in his book Hydrodynamica in 1738.

**CHAPTER 8**

1. Michael Lewis, *Moneyball* (New York: W. W. Norton & Company, 2004).

**CHAPTER 10**

1. Steven Spielberg, *Indiana Jones and the Last Crusade* (Paramount Pictures, 1989).

2. You can learn about Variable Analysis in greater detail at http://www .stopguessingbook.com.

**CHAPTER 11**

1. Stephen King, *On Writing*. (New York: Simon & Schuster, 2001). pg. 275

## ACKNOWLEDGMENTS

I thank the people who have helped me on my problem-solving journey. My mum and dad provided me with many opportunities, and chief among them was encouraging me to question the status quo. This sometimes frustrated people in authority, but it has led me to pay attention to what is going on. I've had many great teachers who have put up with my idiosyncrasies to help me learn how things work. I also appreciate my patient colleagues who have coached me in how to be a better problem-solver, and sometimes simply shown the way with amazing examples of how to crack seemingly impossible problems. Thanks to all of you from the bottom of my heart.

# INDEX

NOTE: Page numbers ending in "n" indicate endnotes.

confidence level for fact-based decisions, 104–105

confirmation bias, opinion-based decisions, 106–107

conflicts of interest, 81–83

consensus opinions, 100

cookies disappearing, example of fact-based decision, 104–105

correlation *vs.* causation, 71–72

curse of knowledge, 83

the curse of luck, 22–23

customer service management, example of fact-based decision, 103–104

## D

decisions. *See* fact-based decisions; opinion-based decisions.

deck, building, 47–48

dental hygiene, 65–66

DePodesta, Paul, 98

diagnosing illnesses, smelling the problem, 29–30

digging into fundamentals
  benefits of, 69–71
  introduction, 63–66
  measurable variables, 66–69
  patterns of failure, 71–73
  relevancy, 66–67

digging into fundamentals, examples. *See also* examples of problems solved.
  avoiding eggs, 73–74
  chemical processing facility, 64–65, 70–71
  cholesterol intake, 73–74
  dental hygiene, 65–66
  food processing plant, 72

lawn care, 67–69

our everyday lives, 73–74

pump seal, 64–65, 70–71

toilets, 63–64

toothpaste, 65

unproductive oil well, 72

weight loss, 73–74

dinosaur hair problem, 44, 45, 54

drywall repair, example, 85

Duhigg, Charles, 66

## E

easy problems, 8–9

eggs, avoiding, 73–74

equipment purchase, complex solutions, 89

examples of problems solved. *See also* smelling the problem, examples.
  box-closing machine, 43–44
  clogged nozzles, 44, 45, 54
  dinosaur hair, 44, 45, 54
  factory machinery in Georgia, 18
  food processing plants. *See* food processing plants, problems solved.
  toilet rolls and shrink wrap, 2–8

examples of problems solved, digging into fundamentals
  avoiding eggs, 73–74
  chemical processing facility, 64–65, 70–71
  cholesterol intake, 73–74
  dental hygiene, 65–66
  food processing plant, 72
  lawn care, 67–69
  our everyday lives, 73–74
  pump seal, 64–65, 70–71

toilets, 63–64
toothpaste, 65
unproductive oil well, 72
weight loss, 73–74
expansiveness, 109–110
experts. *See* relying on experts; SMEs
(subject matter experts).
extreme poverty, problem definition,
51–53

# F

fact-based decisions. *See also*
opinion-based decisions.
confidence level, 104–105
fact finding, 102–103
Oakland Athletics baseball team,
97–98
opinion-based decisions
disguised as, 99–101
opinions *vs.* facts, 105
*vs.* opinions, 98–99
fact-based decisions, examples. *See
also* examples of problems solved.
cookies disappearing, 104–105
customer service management,
103–104
order fulfillment, 103
performance coating company,
103–104
fact finding, fact-based decisions,
102–103
factory machinery in Georgia,
problem, 18
facts *vs.* opinions, 105
Fault Tree Analysis, 25
Five Whys, 12, 25, 131n
focusing on the problem. *See*
problem definition.

food processing plants, problems
solved. *See also* examples of
problems solved.
bottling plant, 35–36
box-closing machine, 43–44
cost of cardboard boxes, 72
making nutritional bars, 60–61
moldy food, 20–22
fundamentals. *See* digging into
fundamentals.

# G

garage door opener, problem,
125–126
The Great Poverty Eradication
Myths, 52
guessing
choosing your method, 118,
120
controlling, 26
the curse of luck, 22–23
in detective work, 22–23
human nature, 26–27
overview, 17–18
in popular problem-solving
methods, 23–25
problem definition, 53–55
reasons for failure, 18–22
Sherlock Holmes, 22
side effects of, 22–23
structured, 21–22
*vs.* simple solutions, 92

# H

hard problems. *See also* complex
solutions.
barriers to solving, 12–13
brainstorming, 20

PTT (push-to-talk), smelling the
problem, 31–32, 81
publicly owned businesses, problem
definition, 58–59
pump seal problem, 64–65, 70–71

## Q

Quan, Mack, 46
questions to ask
to dispel ignorance, 42
problem definition, 61
relying on experts, 84
smelling the problem, 33

## R

rapid answers when relying on
experts, 80–81
red flags for choosing your method,
120–121
relevant facts, identifying, 106
relying on experts
effective use of, 83–86
introduction, 77–79
questions to ask, 84
reasons for, 79–80
SMEs (subject matter experts),
77–79
relying on experts, examples
drywall repair, 85
setting up an LLC (limited
liability company), 82–83
relying on experts, pitfalls of
conflicts of interest, 81–83
curse of knowledge, 83
misalignment, 81–83
opinion-based decisions, 99–101
prejudices, 83

rapid answers, 80–81
risk-reward calculus, 82
wisdom of the group, 99–101
reporting simple solutions, 95–96
risk-reward calculus, 82
root cause analysis
choosing your method, 118
Fault Tree Analysis, 25
Five Whys, 12, 25
guessing, 21–22
PackCorp Scientific Approach,
24–25
*in situ* analysis, 24. *See also*
smelling the problem.

## S

scope
expansiveness, 109–110
lawn care problem, 110–112
mistakes happen, 115–116
problem definition, 58–59
simplifying, 112–115
simple solutions. *See also* complex
solutions.
believing in, 95
introduction, 91
lack of, 94–95
reporting, 95–96
*vs.* guessing, 92
simple solutions, examples
making plastic cosmetic tubes,
94
running out of toilet paper,
92–93
weight loss, 92
simplifying scope, 112–115
Six Sigma techniques, 131n

smelling the problem
    breaking down barriers, 34–35
    building team alignment, 35–36
    developing patterns of failure, 31–33
    end of the process, 36–37
    importance of, 29
    poverty in sub-Saharan Africa, 51–53
    sample questions to ask, 33
    toilet rolls and shrink wrap, 7–8
smelling the problem, examples. *See also* examples of problems solved.
    bottling plant, 35–36
    chemical processing pumps, 34–35
    computer losing power, 33–34
    diagnosing illnesses, 29–30
    push-to-talk feature, 31–32
    toilet rolls and shrink wrap, 6
SMEs (subject matter experts), 77–79. *See also* relying on experts.
solutions. *See* simple solutions.
solving the wrong problem, 54–55. *See also* problem definition.
statistical analysis tools, 106

structured guessing, 21–22
sub-Saharan Africa, problem definition, 51–53

# T

team alignment, building, 35–36
toilet paper running out, simple solution, 92–93
toilet rolls and shrink wrap, problem, 2–8, 114
toilets, digging into fundamentals, 63–64
toothpaste, 65
toothpaste tubes, problem, 47–48
TPS (Toyota Production System), 131n

# V

variable analysis, choosing your method, 122–124

# W

weight loss, 73–74, 92, 100
wisdom of the group, 99–101. *See also* opinion-based decisions.

# ABOUT THE AUTHOR

*Entrepreneur, Abundant Thinker, politics junkie, author, and problem-solver with a burning obsession to routinely do the impossible and unleash the potential of people and systems everywhere.*

Since his youth in Hong Kong, China, Nat has explored various ventures in engineering design, technical problem-solving, organizational transformation, and political reform. The hallmark of each of these efforts is simple: solve the hardest problems that stand between an organization and its best performance.

Problem solving is in Nat's blood. His mother loves to travel and showed Nat how to be fearless when approaching the unknown. In Hong Kong, Nat attended school with classmates from over 40 different countries, speaking 20 different languages. This diversity helped him see how different people approach problems.

Nat's father taught at the University of Hong Kong and has a keen interest in understanding why things fail. As they travelled around the city they would examine corrosion and failing systems; Nat's dad showed him how to identify problems and the damage they caused. Nat chose to study Engineering at Oxford and Cambridge, and then transitioned to become a professional problem-solver. Nat continues to travel, having visited over 50 countries and territories across all seven continents, and lived and worked on three.

Nat sees unsolved problems all around him and laments the missed opportunity to run things better. He believes that the glass is neither half-full nor half-empty, but that there are buckets of opportunity hanging about, waiting to be filled.

In 2001, aged 28, Nat co-founded Stroud International (http://www.stroudinternational.com) and later became CEO. Stroud helps business leaders identify and solve high-value problems that were previously thought to be impossible.

Nat has written *Stop Guessing* to help more people solve hard problems that exist in their businesses, their personal lives, and their community. He hopes to unleash many great problem-solvers through this effort.

At heart, Nat is an adventurer. He was a bungee jump display artist with the Oxford Stunt Factory as an undergraduate, has hiked in the Himalayas, skied to the South Pole, and had to be rescued in the Blackburn Challenge when his double-scull broke in half in the rough Atlantic waters off Cape Ann in Massachusetts. He stays active rowing, skiing, and renovating his home with his family.

In life, he strives everyday to leap out of bed with excitement for what awaits him, and surrounds himself with people that are always teaching and challenging him. Nat is married to his college sweetheart and together they have four children. They live in Marblehead, Massachusetts.

# Berrett–Koehler
## Publishers

# Berrett–Koehler
# Publishers

Connecting people and ideas
to create a world that works for all

Dear Reader,

Thank you for picking up this book and joining our worldwide community of Berrett-Koehler readers. We share ideas that bring positive change into people's lives, organizations, and society.

**To welcome you, we'd like to offer you a free e-book.** You can pick from among twelve of our bestselling books by entering the promotional code **BKP92E** here: http://www.bkconnection.com/welcome.

When you claim your free e-book, we'll also send you a copy of our e-newsletter, the *BK Communiqué*. Although you're free to unsubscribe, there are many benefits to sticking around. In every issue of our newsletter you'll find

- A free e-book
- Tips from famous authors
- Discounts on spotlight titles
- Hilarious insider publishing news
- A chance to win a prize for answering a riddle

Best of all, our readers tell us, "Your newsletter is the only one I actually read." So claim your gift today, and please stay in touch!

Sincerely,

Charlotte Ashlock
Steward of the BK Website

Questions? Comments? Contact me at bkcommunity@bkpub.com.

MIX
Paper from
responsible sources
FSC® C016245

Certified

Corporation
bcorporation.net